A TRANSLATOR'S GUIDE
TO PAUL'S SECOND LETTER
TO THE CORINTHIANS

Helps for Translators Series

Technical Helps:

Old Testament Quotations in the New Testament
Section Headings for the New Testament
Short Bible Reference System
New Testament Index
Orthography Studies
Bible Translations for Popular Use
The Theory and Practice of Translation
Bible Index
Fauna and Flora of the Bible
Short Index to the Bible
Manuscript Preparation
Marginal Notes for the Old Testament
Marginal Notes for the New Testament
The Practice of Translating

Handbooks:

A Translator's Handbook on the Book of Joshua
A Translator's Handbook of the Book of Ruth
A Translator's Handbook on the Book of Amos
A Translator's Handbook on the Books of Obadiah and Micah
A Translator's Handbook on the Book of Jonah
A Translator's Handbook on the Gospel of Mark
A Translator's Handbook on the Gospel of Luke
A Translator's Handbook on the Gospel of John
A Translator's Handbook on the Acts of the Apostles
A Translator's Handbook on Paul's Letter to the Romans
A Translator's Handbook on Paul's Letter to the Galatians
A Translator's Handbook on Paul's Letter to the Ephesians
A Translator's Handbook on Paul's Letter to the Philippians
A Translator's Handbook on Paul's Letters to the Colossians and to Philemon
A Translator's Handbook on Paul's Letters to the Thessalonians
A Translator's Handbook on the First Letter from Peter
A Translator's Handbook on the Letters of John

Guides:

A Translator's Guide to Selections from the First Five Books of the Old Testament
A Translator's Guide to Selected Psalms
A Translator's Guide to the Gospel of Matthew
A Translator's Guide to the Gospel of Mark
A Translator's Guide to the Gospel of Luke
A Translator's Guide to Paul's First Letter to the Corinthians
A Translator's Guide to Paul's Second Letter to the Corinthians

HELPS FOR TRANSLATORS

A TRANSLATOR'S GUIDE
to
PAUL'S SECOND LETTER TO THE CORINTHIANS

by
ROBERT G. BRATCHER

UNITED BIBLE SOCIETIES

London, New York,
Stuttgart

Books in the series of Helps for Translators may be ordered from a national Bible Society or from either of the following centers:

United Bible Societies
European Production Fund
D-7000 Stuttgart 80
Postfach 81 03 40
West Germany

United Bible Societies
1865 Broadway
New York, New York
U.S.A.

L.C. Cataloging in Publication Data

Bratcher, Robert G.
    A translator's guide to Paul's second letter to the Corinthians.

    (Helps for translators)
    Bibliography: p.
    Includes index.
    1. Bible N.T. Corinthians, 2nd—Translating. 2. Bible. N.T. Corinthians, 2nd—Commentaries. I. Title. II. Series.
BS2675.5.B7   1983   227'.307   83-1383
ISBN 0-8267-0186-8 (American Bible Society)

ABS-1983-1500-CM-08571

Contents

Preface

A *Translator's Guide to Paul's Second Letter to the Corinthians* is a continuation of the series of Guides prepared as part of the general series, *Helps for Translators*. The Handbooks were formerly the only exegetical materials on various books of the Bible published by the United Bible Societies for the use of translators.

The Handbooks have proven to be valuable for a good number of translators. They are full-range commentaries that deal with problems of the original text, interpretation, vocabulary analysis, and discourse structure. They also include analysis of translation problems that may occur, and they provide suggestions for dealing with such problems. Some translators, however, prefer material in a more condensed form and from which they can easily retrieve information. Therefore the Translator's Guides do not, for example, attempt in every case to explain the reasons for the exegesis of a passage nor for a suggested solution to a translation problem. A Guide does not take away from translators the responsibility to make their own decisions, but it does attempt to give them practical information and to alert them to pitfalls they may otherwise overlook. It is hoped that such information will enable a translator to prepare a translation that is faithful to the meaning of the original and that is presented in a style which is appropriate and effective in communicating the message to the reader.

Other Guides are in preparation, covering material from both the Old Testament and the New Testament. Meanwhile, preparation of the Handbooks continues, so that the needs of all translators may be met. The United Bible Societies Subcommittee on Translations will welcome any suggestions for making both the Handbooks and the Guides more effective and useful for translators.

Abbreviations Used in This Volume

Books of the Bible

1 Cor	1 Corinthians
2 Cor	2 Corinthians
Deut	Deuteronomy
Exo	Exodus
Gal	Galatians
Heb	Hebrews
Matt	Matthew
Phil	Philippians
Rom	Romans
1 Thes	1 Thessalonians

Other Abbreviations:

A.D.	anno Domini (in the year of our Lord)
KJV	King James Version
RSV	Revised Standard Version
TEV	Today's English Version
UBS	United Bible Societies

Translating Paul's Second Letter to the Corinthians

The purpose of this Guide is to help translators recognize and solve some of the problems they will encounter in translating this Letter. The Guide is not intended to replace standard commentaries or the forthcoming Handbook, which is also to be published by the United Bible Societies. Rather it seeks to show, in a simple and consistent way, what translators must do in order to provide in their own language a text that is faithful to the meaning of the original and that is clear and simple for the reader. Every translator is encouraged to seek additional help from available commentaries and Bible dictionaries, and to consult other translations.

The Letter is divided into sections, each with a heading that indicates the content or the main idea of the section. The translator should carefully read the whole section before starting to translate the first verse of the section.

The Guide uses the Today's English Version (TEV) section headings, and prints the text of the Revised Standard Version (RSV) and of the TEV. The translator will notice that in many places the two are considerably different in form, although in the vast majority of instances the meaning is the same. The differences are due to the fact that the RSV is a translation that tries to reflect, as far as possible, the form of the original Greek, in terms of vocabulary, word classes, word order, and grammatical constructions. The TEV attempts to express the meaning of the Greek text as simply and naturally as possible, using a vocabulary and grammatical constructions that will be easily understood by most people who read English.

The translator is encouraged to imitate the TEV in this respect, and to express the meaning of the text in a form that will be easy for the reader to understand.

After each TEV section heading other suggestions are made for different ways to translate the heading.

After each verse, printed in full in both the RSV (left hand column) and the TEV (right hand column) texts, key passages are selected for explanation; these are underlined, and suggestions are given about other ways of translating. Where necessary, explanations are provided to enable the translator to understand better what is being proposed. Quotations from RSV are underlined, while quotations from TEV and other translations are in quotation marks.

The Guide takes notice of places where there are important differences among the Greek manuscripts of the Letter. In some places RSV and TEV differ in their decision on the Greek text (see 3.2); the Guide states the matter concisely and recommends what a translator should do.

The most important thing is that the translator be thoroughly acquainted with a whole passage (a section or a chapter) before starting to translate it, so as to reflect the author's style, the unity of the passage, and the development of thought.

[1]

THE OCCASION OF THE LETTERS

A translator needs to know something of the time and occasion of Paul's various letters to the Christians in Corinth, since there are references in First and Second Corinthians to other letters he has written. A very brief account of Paul's visits to Corinth and of his letters to the believers there will help the translator to understand the references Paul makes to his past visits to Corinth, his future plans, the missions of Titus and others to Corinth, the plans for raising the relief offering for the needy fellow believers in Judea, and the occasion of Paul's various letters to the Corinthians.

1. Paul's first visit to Corinth is reported in Acts 18.1-18. He arrived there during his second missionary journey and stayed more than eighteen months (Acts 18.11-18). This was probably from spring of A.D. 50 to fall of A.D. 51 (all dates are approximate, and there is no firm agreement on them).

2. In 1 Corinthians 5.9-11 Paul refers to a previous letter he had written the Corinthians, in which he had told them not to tolerate immoral people in their fellowship. This letter has been lost, unless, as some people believe, 2 Corinthians 6.14—7.1 is part of this letter. There is no way of knowing when this first letter was written.

3. The Christians in Corinth wrote Paul a letter and sent it to him by several of their people: perhaps members of the family of Chloe (1 Cor 1.11), and Stephanas, Fortunatus, and Achaicus (1 Cor 16.17-18). They asked Paul's opinion about several problems that were bothering them.

4. Paul answers their letter, writing what we know as First Corinthians. This may have been in A.D. 56 or 57, and he writes from Ephesus (1 Cor 16.8). In the letter he discusses many matters, including the questions that the Corinthians had raised in their letter to him (see 1 Cor 7.1; 7.25; 8.1; 12.1; 16.1; and perhaps 16.12). He sends the letter by Timothy (4.17) and reports that he plans to go from Ephesus to Macedonia, and then on to Corinth (4.19; 16.5-7).

It is clear that Paul's letter did not settle the serious problems which were troubling the church at Corinth. There was sexual immorality, there were factions and divisions in the church, and people had come to Corinth who were trying to take over the leadership of the church. They were criticizing Paul, and trying to get the Corinthians to renounce his leadership.

5. Paul made a quick visit to Corinth, which he describes as sad and painful (he refers to it in 2 Cor 2.1; see also 12.14; 13.1-2). Apparently the visit did not accomplish anything, and Paul returned to Ephesus deeply upset. Before leaving he warned the Corinthians that he would return later and deal decisively with the matter.

6. Back in Ephesus (perhaps still in A.D. 57) Paul wrote a harsh letter to Corinth (see references in 2 Cor 2.3-4,9; 7.8-12). It is clear, from the way in which Paul refers to this letter, that it could not be what we know as 1 Corinthians. This letter greatly upset the Corinthian Christians, but it brought them back to their senses. The letter was taken to Corinth by Titus (see 2 Cor 2.13; 7.13-15). What has happened to this letter? Many believe that chapters 10-13 of 2 Corinthians are the letter, or part of it. If this is true, it helps

explain the surprising change of attitude and tone that Paul shows in
these chapters, as compared with his attitude in chapters 1-9. He is
harsh, critical, sarcastic, and asserts his apostolic authority in the
strongest terms possible. He tells them that he will make his third
visit to Corinth (2 Cor 12.14; 13.1) and will use his apostolic authority fully.

On the assumption that 2 Corinthians 10-13 is (part of) the harsh
letter, it appears that Paul sent the letter to Corinth by Titus (2 Cor
2.13; 7.13-15), with instructions that Titus, after delivering the letter and trying to settle the difficult matters in Corinth, should meet
Paul at Troas. So Paul went there, but he did not meet Titus (2 Cor
2.12-13); he went on to Macedonia (2.13b), and there (perhaps in Philippi) he met Titus (7.5-7; 7.13b), who brought good news from Corinth:
everything had been settled and the Corinthians were anxious to be reconciled with Paul. Paul was overjoyed.

7. In gratitude Paul wrote a thankful, friendly letter. If chapters
10-13 of 2 Corinthians are the harsh letter, this thankful letter is
2 Corinthians 1-9. This would have been written later in A.D. 57, probably in Macedonia (2 Cor 9.2).

He sends the letter to Corinth by Titus and two companions (2 Cor
8.6,16-19,22-24; 9.3-5). The three men are to finish the campaign to
collect funds for the needy Christians in Judea. It is to be noticed
that Titus and another Christian leader, who is not named, had begun
the effort to raise this offering the year before this last letter is
written (see 2 Cor 8.6; 12.18). It is most likely that that visit by
Titus was before he took the harsh letter to Corinth; so this would be
his third visit to the church. Paul himself plans to go to Corinth,
taking along with him some fellow believers from Macedonia, and he
hopes that the offering will be ready when he arrives.

8. Paul makes a last visit to Corinth, staying there for three
months (Acts 20.2-3), at the end of what is known as his third missionary journey. This probably was during the winter of A.D. 57-58.

The evidence in First and Second Corinthians shows that Paul wrote
at least two other letters besides these two. Whether or not the theories are correct which identify 2 Corinthians 6.14—7.1 and chapters
10-13 of 2 Corinthians as part of those other letters, the knowledge
of Paul's various visits and plans will help the translator to understand the change of subject matter, and of Paul's attitude, in First
and Second Corinthians.

OUTLINE OF SECOND CORINTHIANS

Title

SECOND CORINTHIANS

It may be necessary to expand the title somewhat and say "The Second Letter of Paul to the Corinthians" or "The Second Letter that (the Apostle) Paul Wrote to the Church (or, to the Christians) in Corinth." It should be remembered that the title is not part of the original text. Most modern translations do not refer to the apostle as "Saint Paul."

Chapter 1

SECTION HEADING

It is not necessary to use a title as a section heading for the first two verses, but "Introduction" or "Introduction to the Letter" may be used. Or else the section heading appearing in TEV at verse 3 can be placed here.

Paul begins most of his letters to churches in the same way: first he introduces himself and anyone else associated with him as the writer of the letter; then he identifies the people to whom he writes; and lastly he pronounces a short blessing on his readers.

1.1 REVISED STANDARD VERSION

Paul, an apostle of Christ Jesus by the will of God, and Timothy our brother.

To the church of God which is at Corinth, with all the saints who are in the whole of Achaia:

TODAY'S ENGLISH VERSION

From Paul, an apostle of Christ Jesus by God's will, and from our brother Timothy—

To the church of God in Corinth, and to all God's people throughout Achaia:

Paul: it may be necessary to say "I, Paul, who am an apostle..." or "I, Paul, an apostle...write this letter." Or else "This letter is from (or, is written by) Paul...." Modern letters have the name of the writer at the end of the letter, and this could be done for this letter. But the identification of Paul and Timothy as writers of the letter should, in any case, appear here at the beginning.

apostle: a person who has been sent out to speak on behalf of the one who chose him, and to act in his name. An apostle is not simply a messenger but an authorized representative, somewhat like an ambassador.

Christ Jesus: some languages, like Spanish, have the one form "Jesus Christ" as one name (Spanish "Jesuchristo"). But wherever

possible the order <u>Christ Jesus</u> should be followed. Here <u>Christ</u> is no
longer a title but a proper name.

    <u>by the will of God</u>: "because God decided," "because God wanted
him to."

    <u>Timothy</u>: one of Paul's younger colleagues, who traveled with him
and helped him in the work (see Acts 16.1-4; Phil 2.19-22).

    <u>our brother</u>: the Greek says simply "the brother," but in transla-
tion the inclusive first person plural pronoun <u>our</u> is recommended;
"our Christian brother," "our fellow believer."

    <u>the church of God</u>: the basic element of <u>church</u> in the New Testa-
ment is people, not a building or an institution; and some translators
have used expressions such as "God's people," or "the congregation of
God's people," or "the people who belong to God."

    <u>Corinth</u> was the capital city of the Roman province of <u>Achaia</u>,
which corresponded to what is now southern Greece. For Paul's work in
Corinth see Acts 18.1-18.

    <u>the saints</u>: "the people of God." The word which in the Old Testa-
ment is used of the people of Israel is used in the New Testament of
the followers of Jesus Christ, the new people of God. There is no difference in meaning between <u>the church of God</u> and <u>the saints</u>; both refer
to the Christians.

    <u>Achaia</u>: it may be better to identify it as a province, "the prov-
ince of Achaia"; it should be made clear that the city of Corinth was
in the province of Achaia.

    Verse 1 may be translated as follows:

        I, Paul, am an apostle sent out by (or, representing)
    Christ Jesus because God so decided. Our Christian brother
    Timothy and I write this letter to God's people in the city
    of Corinth, and also to all other Christian believers in
    the province of Achaia.

1.2	RSV	TEV
	Grace to you and peace from God our Father and the Lord Jesus Christ.	May God our Father and the Lord Jesus Christ give you grace and peace.

    <u>Grace...and peace</u>: these two words are standard in the letters
of Paul. <u>Grace</u> means God's favor, good will, blessing; and <u>peace</u> means
not just a lack of conflict, but the sense of well-being which results
from the proper relationship that God's people have with God and with
one another.

    <u>our Father</u>: here <u>our</u> is inclusive, meaning all Christians.

    It is better to make a complete sentence of verse 2, either as
TEV does, or else as follows: "I pray that God our Father and the Lord
Jesus Christ will bless you and give you peace (or, spiritual well-
being)."

SECTION HEADING

Paul Gives Thanks to God: "Paul's Prayer of Thanksgiving," "Paul Thanks God for His Help."

In this prayer of thanksgiving, verses 3-11, Paul emphasizes how God has helped and comforted him in his sufferings, and that God can and will do the same for the Christians in Corinth. Actually the prayer occupies only verses 3-4; the rest of the section describes the sufferings and difficulties of Paul and his companions. So the section heading could be "Suffering and Consolation (or, Help)."

Paul does not praise the Corinthian Christians for helping him, but shows how his own experience is of help to them. So their experience will be like his, and the result will be many prayers of thanks to God.

1.3	RSV	TEV
	Blessed be the God and Father of our Lord Jesus Christ, the Father of mercies and God of all comfort,	Let us give thanks to the God and Father of our Lord Jesus Christ, the merciful Father, the God from whom all help comes!

Blessed be: RSV follows the form of the Greek text, without a stop until the end of verse 4. The Hebrew expression translated Blessed be means "Let us praise (or, give thanks)." In the Bible, "to bless God" means to praise him; it does not mean to confer blessings on God, but to thank him for his blessings. "We must all thank God" or "Praise (or, Thanks) be to God."

the God and Father of our Lord Jesus Christ: here God is described in terms of his relation to Jesus Christ, who is the Lord of all believers. It may be better to say "Thanks be to God, who is the God and Father of Jesus Christ, our Lord."

the Father of mercies and God of all comfort: the two phrases have almost the same meaning. The first one means "the Father (or, our Father) who is merciful (or, kind, or, compassionate)"; the second means "the God who supplies (or, from whom comes) all comfort." The plural mercies reflects the Hebrew form; it does not mean separate acts of kindness but a constant attitude.

Comfort translates a Greek word which carries not only the sense of consoling someone in trouble, that is, cheering him up, making him feel better, but also the active idea of help or encouragement. So TEV has "the God from whom all help comes"; or it could be "the God who is always ready to help us," "the God who always strengthens us." It should be noticed that in verses 3-7 the verb and the noun "comfort" occur a total of ten times, which indicates the importance of the subject as Paul writes to the Corinthian Christians.

1.4	RSV	TEV
	who comforts us in all our affliction, so that we may be able	He helps us in all our troubles, so that we are able to help others

to comfort those who are in any affliction, with the comfort with which we ourselves are comforted by God.	who have all kinds of troubles, using the same help that we ourselves have received from God.

RSV translates literally the three times the verb <u>comfort</u> occurs, and the one time the noun appears in this verse. TEV has tried to use a more natural form of English. TEV has also made a complete sentence of verse 4. Another way of beginning verse 4 is "It is he who helps us...."

<u>us...our...we</u>: these pronouns could be taken as referring only to Paul (and Timothy); but they probably refer to all who do the kind of work that Paul and Timothy do.

<u>affliction</u>: "trouble," "difficulty," "hardship." Paul is thinking of the difficulties and troubles he faces in his work as an apostle.

The repetition of the idea of comfort makes for a rather involved sentence, and a structure different from TEV might be better: "He helps us in all our troubles. And so, with this help that God has given us, we are able to help others who have troubles." Or "He helps us in all our troubles, and we are able to use that same help in order to help others who are in any kind of trouble."

1.5 RSV	TEV
For as we share abundantly in Christ's sufferings, so through Christ we share abundantly in comfort too.*a*	Just as we have a share in Christ's many sufferings, so also through Christ we share in God's great help.
*a*Or, *For as the sufferings of Christ abound for us, so also our comfort abounds through Christ*	

The sufferings and the encouragement which Paul and his colleagues experience are actually a sharing in the sufferings of Christ and in the encouragement that he supplies.

<u>we share abundantly in Christ's sufferings</u>: the idea of sharing Christ's suffering may be difficult if not impossible to express, especially if it appears that Paul is saying that they suffered at the same time that Christ did, and in the same way. For Paul the only explanation was this: because of their union with Christ, he and his companions suffered, as Christ had suffered, and they were also helped, as Christ was helped. It may be necessary to express the meaning as follows: "Christ suffered, and we also suffer as he did; and as Christ was helped by God, so by means of Christ we are helped by God."

It is difficult to understand the alternative rendering in the RSV footnote; it is a formal representation of the Greek text and is not normal English.

1.6 RSV

If we are afflicted, it is for
your comfort and salvation; and
if we are comforted, it is for
your comfort, which you experience
when you patiently endure the same
sufferings that we suffer.

TEV

If we suffer, it is for your help
and salvation; if we are helped,
then you too are helped and given
the strength to endure with patience the same sufferings that
we also endure.

Here Paul begins to distinguish between himself and his companions (we), and his readers (your...you).

If we are afflicted: the conditional If does not imply any doubt about the suffering; it is simply a way of stating the case. The trans-lation could be "Whenever we suffer"; "Every time we suffer"; or "Be-cause we suffer, you receive help and salvation...."

afflicted: RSV reflects the use of two different words in verses 4-6 in Greek: affliction (and afflicted) and sufferings (and suffer). The two mean the same and TEV uses the same English word in all cases.

salvation: here in the sense of spiritual well-being. The Christian faith of the readers will be sustained throughout their sufferings; they will not give up. The sufferings of Paul and his companions benefit the Corinthian Christians.

In the same way, if we are comforted, then the readers will also be helped.

it is for your comfort: TEV "then you too are helped." What follows (which you experience) may also be rendered: "then you too are helped by being enabled (or, by being given the strength) to endure with pa-tience...." It would seem that instead of RSV (comfort,) which you ex-perience, the Greek text means "(comfort,) which enables you (to endure patiently)...."

the same sufferings that we suffer: that is, the same kinds of sufferings, or "to suffer in the same way."

The verse may be translated as follows:

Whenever we suffer, you receive help and are strengthened spiritually; and whenever we are helped (by God), you re-ceive the same help, which makes you able to endure pa-tiently the same kind of sufferings that we experience.

TEXTUAL NOTE: Verse 6 in the Textus Receptus (of which the King James Version [KJV] is a translation) has no basis in any known Greek manuscript.

1.7 RSV

Our hope for you is unshaken; for
we know that as you share in our
sufferings, you will also share
in our comfort.

TEV

So our hope in you is never shaken;
we know that just as you share in
our sufferings, you also share in
the help we receive.

Our hope for you is unshaken: "So we never give up our hope for you." In the New Testament, hope is often, as here, practically equiva-lent to confidence, assurance. Here the translation could be "So we never lose our confidence in you" or "So we are always sure (or, confi-dent) about you."

as you share in our sufferings: "just as you have suffered (or, you suffer) as we have," "just as you have experienced the same kind of sufferings that we have experienced."

you will also share: there is no verb in Greek, and it is probable that TEV is correct, "you also share."

1.8	RSV	TEV
	For we do not want you to be ignorant, brethren, of the affliction we experienced in Asia; for we were so utterly, unbearably crushed that we despaired of life itself.	We want to remind you, brothers, of the trouble we had in the province of Asia. The burdens laid upon us were so great and so heavy that we gave up all hope of staying alive.

we do not want you to be ignorant: "we want you to know," "we want you to realize (or, to remember)."

brethren: "fellow believers," "brothers and sisters," "fellow Christians." Paul did not intend to omit the women believers from his letter, so a translation is justified in using a term that includes men and women.

affliction: "trouble" (TEV), "difficulty," "suffering."

we experienced: it is quite possible that here Paul is speaking of himself alone, and some translations use the first person singular "I experienced."

Asia is the Roman province of Asia, in what is now western Turkey; its capital city was Ephesus.

we were so utterly, unbearably crushed: Paul uses figurative language and speaks of his troubles as "burdens" laid on him, which almost killed him. There is no indication what kind of intense difficulty or suffering this was.

The verse may be translated:

We want to remind you, our brothers and sisters, of the great troubles we had in the province of Asia. They were so great that we lost all hope of staying alive.

1.9	RSV	TEV
	Why, we felt that we had received the sentence of death; but that was to make us rely not on ourselves but on God who raises the dead;	We felt that the death sentence had been passed on us. But this happened so that we should rely, not on ourselves, but only on God, who raises the dead.

we felt that we had received the sentence of death: "we were convinced that we were going to die." It would not seem that the sentence of death is here used in the legal sense of a sentence handed down by a judge. Rather it would seem that this is figurative language: death seemed as inevitable as it would be if Paul had been sentenced to death by a court.

that (in but that was): the conviction that death was certain.

to make us rely not on ourselves but on God: or "to keep us from relying on ourselves, but to rely only on God," or "so that we should not rely on ourselves, but rely only on God."

God who raises the dead: "God, who brings dead people back to life" or "...who causes the dead to live again," "...who resurrects the dead." This is the greatest demonstration of God's power: he can overcome even the greatest of all dangers and protect his faithful servants.

1.10 RSV	TEV
he delivered us from so deadly a peril, and he will deliver us; on him we have set our hope that he will deliver us again.	From such terrible dangers of death*a* he saved us, and will save us; and we have placed our hope in him that he will save us again,
	*a*terrible dangers of death; *some manuscripts have* terrible death.

so deadly a peril: "such great danger," "such dangerous peril." The Greek text is uncertain here. RSV and the TEV footnote translate one form of the text; the TEV text "terrible dangers of death" translates another form of the Greek text. The translation of this text could be "such mortal (or, deadly) dangers." There is no way to decide which is correct; the translator should feel free to follow either RSV or TEV in deciding on which Greek text to translate.

he will deliver us...he will deliver us again: the repetition of the future "he will save us" seems rather strange, and some Greek manuscripts and ancient versions have "he saves us" instead of the first "he will save us." But it is quite clear that this was a change made by copyists.

on him we have set our hope: as seen in verse 7, hope is often the equivalent of "confidence," and here the translation can be "and we have confidence in him."

The verse may be translated as follows:
In the past he saved us from such deadly dangers (or, from such a terrible death), and he will save us in the future. And we have confidence in him that he will continue to save us.

1.11 RSV	TEV
You also must help us by prayer, so that many will give thanks on our behalf for the blessing granted us in answer to many prayers.	as you help us by means of your prayers for us. So it will be that the many prayers for us will be answered, and God will bless us; and many will raise their voices to him in thanksgiving for us.

You also must help us: this translates a participle in Greek, which often has the force of an imperative. But it seems likely that TEV is more accurate in translating "as you help us." That is, the participle indicates means or attendant circumstances; or it can be taken to mean "if you help us...."

so that: this indicates the result of the prayers of the believers in Corinth on behalf of Paul (and of his companions).

It is to be noticed that there are three actions, which are given in reverse order in the text. The chronological order is as follows: (1) many people pray on behalf of Paul and his companions; (2) God answers their prayers and blesses Paul and his companions; (3) many people thank God for blessing the apostles. TEV has arranged the actions in their proper order, for greater ease of understanding. It might be simpler to translate "Many people will pray (to God) for us, and God will answer their prayers and bless us. And so many (others) will thank God for blessing us."

SECTION HEADING

The Change in Paul's Plans: "Paul Explains Why He Changed His Plans."

Paul continues reviewing the past events in his relationship with the church in Corinth and explains his recent actions and his change of plans. Paul emphasizes that he had been honest and straightforward in what he had done, and had not tried to deceive them. Evidently there was a lot of trouble between Paul and the Corinthian Christians, and Paul is doing his best to remedy the situation. In verses 12-14 Paul begins talking directly about his relationship with the Corinthians, which leads to a discussion in verses 15 and following of his change of plans.

1.12 RSV	TEV
For our boast is this, the testimony of our conscience that we have behaved in the world, and still more toward you, with holiness and godly sincerity, not by earthly wisdom but by the grace of God.	We are proud that our conscience assures us that our lives in this world, and especially our relations with you, have been ruled by God-given frankness[b] and sincerity, by the power of God's grace and not by human wisdom.
	[b]frankness; *some manuscripts have* holiness.

our boast is this: the first person plural pronoun is still used; only at verse 15 does Paul begin to use the singular pronoun. Some translations may wish to begin the use of the singular here in verse 12, since Paul seems to be referring to himself alone.

RSV translates the Greek text literally, the testimony of our conscience, without providing a logical connection with what precedes. TEV "We are proud that our conscience assures us..." tries to express the meaning in normal English style.

conscience: a way of speaking of a person's inner sense about the moral quality of an action or attitude. It is regarded as an independent agent which is able to judge the rightness or wrongness of an action or attitude.

To speak of the testimony of our conscience may be difficult, if not impossible, in many languages. So the translation may say "This is what we are proud of: our conscience tells us..." or "We are proud of the fact that our conscience assures us...." If it is impossible to think of a person's conscience speaking to that person or telling that person something, it may be necessary to translate "We are proud of the way we have behaved (or, acted); we have no doubt (or, we are certain) that our lives in this world...."

we have behaved in the world: it seems certain that by in the world Paul is talking about activities and relationships involving other people, including non-Christians, as contrasted with those involving the Corinthian Christians (still more toward you).

we have behaved...with holiness and godly sincerity: RSV follows a Greek text which has the word for "holiness"; TEV follows a text which has the word for "frankness." The manuscript evidence is not decisive, and neither is the internal evidence, that is, the evidence to be gathered from the writer's style or the development of the subject in the passage in which the word is used. The word holiness is not used anywhere else by Paul; however, the Greek word meaning "frankness" (or "generosity") appears elsewhere in this letter in 8.2; 9.11,13; 11.3. If the translator follows RSV, holiness can be represented by "pure" or "virtuous"; if TEV is preferred which seems better, "single-ness of purpose," "pure motives," "honesty," can be used. Joined with the following word sincerity, the two characterize Paul's conduct as aboveboard, pure, genuine, without guile or duplicity.

RSV takes godly to modify only sincerity; TEV takes it to modify both nouns: "God-given frankness and sincerity"; or "the honesty and sincerity that God demands" or "...that God wants."

earthly wisdom...grace of God: these two are contrasted as the two possible influences which might have determined Paul's conduct.

earthly wisdom (TEV "human wisdom") translates the phrase "carnal (or, fleshly) wisdom," which refers to wisdom apart from God, merely human in source and content, and not determined by divine wisdom.

God's grace is his love in action, leading and helping his servants to do his will.

The verse may be translated:

One thing we are proud of, and are very sure of: we have always behaved ourselves, especially in our relations with you, with the honesty and sincerity that God demands. We have not been guided by our own (human) wisdom, but by the power of God's grace.

1.13-14	RSV	TEV
	For we write you nothing but what you can read and understand; I hope you will understand fully, 14 as you have understood in part,	We write to you only what you can read and understand. But even though you now understand us only in part, I hope that you will

that you can be proud of us as we can be of you, on the day of the Lord Jesus.

come to understand us completely, so that in the Day of our Lord Jesus you can be as proud of us as we shall be of you.

In these two verses Paul refers explicitly to his letters. He supports his claim that he is perfectly sincere and open by calling attention to his letters: there is nothing ambiguous or misleading in them. His meaning is transparently clear, and he is not trying to deceive anyone.

nothing but what: the negative form is emphatic, but it may be more natural in some languages to use a positive form: "You are able to read and understand everything we write," "All our letters to you are easy to read and understand."

you will understand fully, as you have understood in part: here you have understood seems to refer to a time in the recent past when there was some misunderstanding on the part of the Corinthians. The translation could be "you did not understand us (or, me) completely." Or else, as TEV translates, this may refer to the present situation: the Corinthians do not now completely understand Paul's action, but he hopes that in the future they will do so.

proud: pride may seem unworthy of a Christian, but Paul often speaks of boasting, or of being full of pride, or of being proud. For him there is room for a believer's pride, when it results from the actions of God and Christ. In some languages pride may be something completely bad, and "boasting" may be the same as empty bragging. So it may be necessary to speak of "being very glad" about something, or "satisfied" or "contented," or even, at times, "to be grateful" or "to be gratified."

TEV rearranges the material and translates the two verses 13 and 14 as one unit; RSV reflects the order of the Greek text.

on the day of the Lord Jesus: this is the final Day of Judgment, when all people will be judged by God and Christ. It may be translated "on the day when our Lord Jesus returns" or "on the day when our Lord Jesus will judge all people." It is to be noticed that RSV has the Lord Jesus while TEV has "our Lord Jesus." TEV follows the text of the United Bible Societies' (UBS) Greek New Testament.

Verses 13-14 may be translated as follows:
Our letters to you are always easy to read and to understand (or, are always clear and simple). At the present time, however, you don't understand us completely, but I hope that in the future you will understand us completely. Then on the day our Lord Jesus Christ returns (to judge all people), you will be as proud of us as we shall be of you.

1.15	RSV	TEV

1.15   RSV   TEV

Because I was sure of this, I wanted to come to you first, so that you might have a double pleasure;*b*

I was so sure of all this that I made plans at first to visit you, in order that you might be blessed twice.

*b*Other ancient authorities read *favor*

I was sure of this: that is, that the Corinthians would fully understand Paul's motives and purpose.

I wanted to come to you first: or "I made plans at first to visit you" (TEV). It would appear that TEV "at first" is more probable in the context than RSV come to you first—that is, the text doesn't mean that Paul was planning to visit the Corinthians before he went elsewhere, but that his original plan had been to go to Corinth and return the same way (verse 16). But he had to change his plan (verse 23).

a double pleasure: this translates one form of the Greek text; TEV "be blessed twice" and the RSV footnote "(a double) favor" translate another form. The text translated by TEV seems to have stronger manuscript support. If the RSV text is followed, the translation could be "you might be made happy two times"; if TEV is followed, "you might be benefited two times." TEV "be blessed" takes the Greek word to mean God's favor; but it probably means a human favor, or gift, or benefit.

1.16 RSV	TEV
I wanted to visit you on my way to Macedonia, and to come back to you from Macedonia and have you send me on my way to Judea.	For I planned to visit you on my way to Macedonia and again on my way back, in order to get help from you for my trip to Judea.

I wanted to visit you: as the context makes clear, Paul was not able to carry out his original plan.

on my way to Macedonia: Macedonia was a Roman province covering what is now mostly northern Greece; its capital city was Thessalonica. It is assumed that Paul had been in Ephesus when he made that plan to go through Corinth on his way to Macedonia.

have you send me on my way: the Greek verb "to send on" may have the additional meaning of helping with the expenses of the trip; and it seems likely that this is the meaning here. So TEV translates "to get help from you for my trip to Judea." This trip to Judea was for the purpose of taking the contributions from the churches to the needy fellow Christians in Jerusalem.

This verse may be translated as follows: "I was planning to visit you on my way to Macedonia, and again on my return from there (or, from Macedonia). At that time you could help me on my trip to Judea."

1.17 RSV	TEV
Was I vacillating when I wanted to do this? Do I make my plans like a worldly man, ready to say Yes and No at once?	In planning this, did I appear fickle? When I make my plans, do I make them from selfish motives, ready to say "Yes, yes" and "No, no" at the same time?

Paul here denies he changed his plans for no reason at all; it would seem that this is what his opponents in Corinth were saying.

vacillating: "hesitating," "going back and forth," "without really intending to do what I had planned."

when I wanted to do this: or "In planning this" (TEV). The Greek is concise but the context is clear: the accusation that Paul was fickle was not made against him when he first planned his visit but later, when he had to change his plans. Consequently some translations make this quite explicit here, as follows: "Was I being fickle when I changed (or, had to change) my plans?" A translation is justified in expressing this implied meaning quite clearly.

The question is a way of making a statement. Paul affirms that he was not being fickle; he was honest and serious about his plans. "I was not being irresponsible (or, fickle) when I changed my plans."

like a worldly man: this translates the Greek phrase "according to the flesh"; TEV "from selfish motives." Other translations could be "from unworthy motives," "like a man with no moral standards," "like an unprincipled man."

ready to say Yes and No at once?: or, better, "ready to say 'Yes' and 'No' at the same time?" or "ready to change my 'Yes' to 'No' without hesitation?"

1.18   RSV   TEV
As surely as God is faithful, our   As surely as God speaks the truth,
word to you has not been Yes and   my promise to you was not a "Yes"
No.   and a "No."

As surely as God is faithful: Paul takes a solemn vow, appealing to God's own unchanging nature, as he affirms that he (and his companions) has always been honest and consistent in his dealings with the Corinthians. "As surely as God speaks the truth" (TEV) or "As surely as God is true." It may be difficult to represent such a vow, or oath, in the way it is done in Greek or English. So a translation may have to say "God is always true (or, always speaks the truth). In the same way I speak the truth as I say that...."

our word to you: it is to be noticed that the Greek here uses the first person plural; it may be that Paul is now including his companions in what he says. Here word may mean specifically "promise" (TEV) or "message," that is, the Christian message. In the context, it would seem that the Greek phrase is quite general and means "what we (or, I) say (or, have said) to you."

has not been Yes and No: or "does not change from Yes to No," or "is not a Yes and a No at the same time." Paul denies any inconsistency or fickleness.

1.19   RSV   TEV
For the Son of God, Jesus Christ,   For Jesus Christ, the Son of God,
whom we preached among you, Silva-   who was preached among you by
nus and Timothy and I, was not Yes   Silas, Timothy, and myself, is
and No; but in him it is always   not one who is "Yes" and "No." On
Yes.   the contrary, he is God's "Yes";

Paul now appeals to Jesus Christ, that is, to the Christian message about him.

whom we preached among you: it may not be possible to speak of "preaching" a person, but only a message about a person. So here it may be necessary to say "Silvanus, Timothy, and I proclaimed among you the message about Jesus Christ, the Son of God. And that message is not a Yes and a No at the same time (or, that message does not change from Yes to No)." But if Jesus Christ can function as the direct object of the verb, then the translation could be: "Silvanus, Timothy, and I proclaimed among you Jesus Christ, the Son of God; and he is not 'Yes' and 'No' at the same time" or "...is not one who changes from 'Yes' to 'No.'"

Silvanus is the alternate form of "Silas" (TEV), the more familiar name of Paul's companion (see Acts 15.22—18.5).

in him it is always Yes: Jesus Christ is the one who faithfully and truly represents God's will and purpose. Here Jesus is spoken of as the firm guarantee of God's promises to his people; so it is better, with TEV and others, to translate "On the contrary, he is always God's 'Yes.'"

1.20 RSV	TEV
For all the promises of God find their Yes in him. That is why we utter the Amen through him, to the glory of God.	for it is he who is the "Yes" to all of God's promises. This is why through Jesus Christ our "Amen" is said to the glory of God.

find their Yes: that is, Christ is the guarantee, the proof, that God does what he promises his people. If possible the same use of "Yes" should continue in translation: "for it is he who is the 'Yes' to all of God's promises" (TEV). What God promises he fulfills through Jesus Christ.

Amen: this is the equivalent of the Hebrew word which means "may it be so" or "it is so," "indeed," used at the close of prayer by those present, to show that they agree and affirm the prayer as their own.

we utter...through him: here is the equivalent of "in his name." "That is why we say 'Amen' in his name" (or, "in the name of Jesus Christ"). The we here is probably inclusive, that is, it includes all Christians.

for the glory of God: this may mean, as RSV and TEV have it, that the Amen is said in Christ's name in order to bring glory to God. But the phrase may mean "when we praise God," and the translation may be as follows: "That is why we always say 'Amen' in the name of Jesus Christ when (or, every time that) we praise God."

1.21-22 RSV	TEV
But it is God who establishes us with you in Christ, and has commissioned us; 22 he has put his seal upon us and given us his Spirit in our hearts as a guarantee.	It is God himself who makes us, together with you, sure of our life in union with Christ; it is God himself who has set us apart, 22 who has placed his mark of

[17]

> ownership upon us, and who has
> given us the Holy Spirit in our
> hearts as the guarantee of all
> that he has in store for us.

Four things are said in these two verses about what God has done
to and for the apostles: he establishes us, he has commissioned us, he
has put his seal on us, and he has given us his Spirit.

The first verb means "to make firm," "to make solid (or, sure)."
Here it may mean to confirm the relationship which Paul and his companions, together with his readers, have with Christ (TEV "our life in
union with Christ"; RSV in Christ); so the translation can be "God
assures us that we, together with you, belong to Christ" or "God keeps
us, together with you, firmly united to Christ" or "...makes us faithful followers of Christ."

The second verb (commissioned) means literally "to anoint"; and
here it seems to mean "to choose" or "to authorize," "to set apart"
(TEV) as apostles of Christ. Elsewhere in the New Testament the verb
is used only of Christ as "the anointed One" of God. The translation
can be: "God...set us apart (or, chose us) for our work."

he has put his seal on us: this indicates ownership, so TEV has
"who has placed his mark of ownership upon us." Or else, "who has
marked us as his own." In later times the Greek noun "seal" was used
of baptism, and some scholars see that meaning here. This is possible
but does not seem probable.

Here and in the following statement, us is inclusive—it includes
all believers.

has...given us his Spirit...as a guarantee: the Greek word translated guarantee was used in commercial transactions to mean the down
payment which the buyer made on the purchase of some item. This down
payment was a guarantee that the rest of the price would be fully paid.
In the same way, Paul is saying that the Holy Spirit, whom God gives
to believers at the start of their Christian life, is a first installment, a guarantee that God will give all the other blessings that he
has promised. So TEV translates "as the guarantee of all that he has
in store for us." Others translate "as an installment and pledge of
what is to come."

in our hearts: "in our soul," "in our spirit"—or whatever else
is appropriate for an inner spiritual experience.

1.23	RSV	TEV
	But I call God to witness against me—it was to spare you that I refrained from coming to Corinth.	I call God as my witness—he knows my heart! It was in order to spare you that I decided not to go to Corinth.

I call God to witness against me: Paul uses the language of the
law court to emphasize that he is speaking the truth in what he says.
It is not certain that the Greek means (witness) against me; it may
mean simply "I call God as my witness." Or else, as TEV translates,
the Greek phrase "upon my soul" may be a shorthand way of saying "as

one who knows my inmost thoughts." Many translate the phrase "I stake my life on it," and this may be the best way to translate it.

Paul is very emphatic; he wants to impress his readers with the explanation of why he changed his plans and did not go to Corinth.

to spare you: "to keep from upsetting you," "so as not to cause you any more trouble."

1.24 RSV	TEV
Not that we lord it over your faith; we work with you for your joy, for you stand firm in your faith.	We are not trying to dictate to you what you must believe; we know that you stand firm in the faith. Instead, we are working with you for your own happiness.

Not that we lord it over your faith: it is better to make a complete sentence in translation; for example: "Our purpose (or, desire) is not to be in control of you and tell you what you should believe"; or else, as TEV has it, "We are not trying to dictate to you what you must believe," or "We do not want to dictate...."

we work with you for your joy: "we want to work with you so that you will be happy" or "...will be even happier."

For you stand firm in your faith goes with the first part of the verse, as an explanation of why Paul does not presume to tell them what they must believe (see TEV). It may not be possible to use the figure of stand firm; so the translation may be "for your faith is strong (or, mature)," "for you are sure about what you believe" or "you have no doubts about what you should believe."

Chapter 2

2.1   RSV

For I made up my mind not to make
you another painful visit.

TEV

So I made up my mind not to
come to you again to make you sad.

For: the logic of the statement demands "So" (TEV), "For this reason," "Therefore."

another painful visit: that is, another visit that would cause
pain to the Corinthians. This makes clear that Paul had already made
a visit to them which brought sadness both to the Corinthians and to
Paul. He wanted to avoid another such unpleasant experience. The translation could be "And so I firmly decided that I would not make another
visit to you that would make you (and me) sad."

2.2   RSV

For if I cause you pain, who is
there to make me glad but the one
whom I have pained?

TEV

For if I were to make you sad,
who would be left to cheer me up?
Only the very persons I had made
sad.

This rhetorical question, introduced by a conditional statement
(if I cause you pain) is Paul's way of showing the Corinthians how
foolish it would be for him to visit them again when the result would
only be sadness and pain, not happiness.

For if I cause you pain: instead of a condition (also TEV "For if
I were to make you sad"), a statement of fact may be made: "My visit
to you would only make you (and me) sad."

who is there...?: this is Paul's way of saying that there would
be no one left to cheer him up except the very ones (that is, the Corinthians) whom he, Paul, had saddened. It is to be noticed that the
Greek has the singular the one whom I have pained. Many believe the
singular is simply a way of referring to the Corinthians as a whole,
not to one particular person; see the plural those who in the next
verse. So TEV has here in verse 2 "the very persons."

The verse may be translated as follows:

My visit to you would only make you sad (or, cause you
pain). And so there would be no one to cheer me up, because all of you would be sad.

2.3   RSV

And I wrote as I did, so that I
might not suffer pain from those
who should have made me rejoice,

TEV

That is why I wrote that letter
to you—I did not want to come
to you and be made sad by the

for I felt sure of all of you,
that my joy would be the joy of
you all.

very people who should make me
glad. For I am convinced that
when I am happy, then all of you
are happy too.

I wrote: this and I wrote in verse 4 refer to a letter Paul wrote
the Corinthians before the letter he is writing now. As the text says,
Paul was very sad when he wrote the previous letter, and it made the
Corinthians sad (see also 2.9; 7.8,12). The letter we call 1 Corinthians
does not fit that description, and it seems very likely that there was
another letter, which has not been preserved (unless, as some believe,
chapters 10-13 of 2 Corinthians are that letter, or at least part of
it).

And I wrote as I did: implicit in this is the alternative course
of action "That is why I wrote that letter to you instead of visiting
you." Paul canceled his visit and, instead, wrote the Corinthians a
letter. It is possible, however, that the meaning is "That is why I
wrote in that letter that I did not want to visit you then." But the
other seems preferable.

Instead of RSV when I came, it is better to translate, with TEV,
"I did not want to come."

I might not suffer pain from those who should have made me rejoice:
"I did not want to be saddened by the very people who should make me
feel glad." Or it might be better to change the order of the clauses
and make the statement more personal: "I did not want to visit you, for
my meeting with you would only make me sad. And you are the ones who
should make me happy!"

for I felt sure of all of you: here Paul goes on to explain to the
Corinthian Christians that he is certain that when he is happy, they
also are happy. Both in terms of sadness and happiness, Paul is stressing how closely he and his readers are joined in Christian love and
fellowship. His language is not always easy to understand, and it reflects deep distress on his part.

Verse 3 may be translated:
The reason why I wrote that letter was that I did not want
to visit you. For a visit at that time would only make me
sad. And you are the very people who should make me glad!
And I am certain that when I am happy, all of you are happy
too.

2.4	RSV	TEV
	For I wrote you out of much afflic- tion and anguish of heart and with many tears, not to cause you pain but to let you know the abundant love that I have for you.	I wrote you with a greatly troubled and distressed heart and with many tears; my purpose was not to make you sad, but to make you realize how much I love you all.

much affliction...anguish of heart...many tears: Paul describes
his deep distress when he wrote the previous letter. There are various
ways in which to describe these emotions: "I was very sad and deeply
distressed, and was (actually) crying when I wrote that letter." Or,

"When I wrote that letter I was so unhappy and upset that I was crying."
The Greek phrase translated anguish of heart (TEV "distressed heart")
means distress, anxiety, pain; see the English phrase "a heavy heart."

not to cause you pain: "I did not write in order to make you sad,"
"It was not to make you sad that I wrote you." Or else, "My purpose in
writing you was not to make you sad, but so that you would know how
much I love you."

SECTION HEADING

Forgiveness for the Offender: "The Person Who Offended Paul Should
Be Forgiven," "Paul Forgives the Man Who Offended Him."

In this short section, Paul refers in a rather indirect way to
past events involving a person in the church in Corinth who had offended
him. Of course the incident was well known to Paul and to his readers,
so he doesn't have to be explicit and detailed in his comments.

2.5 RSV	TEV
But if any one has caused pain, he has caused it not to me, but in some measure—not to put it too severely—to you all.	Now, if anyone has made somebody sad, he has not done it to me but to all of you—in part, at least. (I say this because I do not want to be too hard on him.)

if any one has caused pain: again Paul writes in a conditional
form. It is a tactful way of referring to a very disagreeable episode,
and Paul does not wish to make matters any worse. The translation can
be in the form of a statement: "The man (or, person) who was the cause
of pain (or, of offense) did not really cause me pain (or, offend me)."
Or else, speaking in an impersonal way, "The injury that has been
caused has not hurt me." The pain ("sadness," see TEV) that the Corinthian Christian caused was the result of a controversy in which Paul
had evidently been accused of being either deceitful, at the worst, or
at least inconsistent. Paul shows that the greater injury was done to
the whole congregation in Corinth and not just to himself. But he tactfully qualifies his charge; it would seem that not all of the church
members in Corinth felt that the man's words or conduct had been of-
fensive.

TEV seems clearer than RSV: "...he has not done it to me but to
all of you—in part, at least."

not to put it too severely: or "I don't want to exaggerate" or "I
do not wish to overstress the matter." TEV "I say this" makes it easier
to understand what Paul means. And TEV "I do not want to be too hard on
him" takes the Greek verb (which has no object in the Greek text) to
refer explicitly to the offender: Paul does not want to be too severe
in his condemnation of the man.

in some measure...to you all: Paul does not say that everyone in
the church at Corinth was against what the man had said and done. So
a translation could say "but at least to some, if not all, of you."

The verse may be translated:
The hurt (or, pain) that has been caused was not to me but
to you; or, at least, to some of you. I do not want to be
too hard on the man who caused it (or, I don't want to exaggerate the matter).

2.6 RSV	TEV
For such a one this punishment by the majority is enough;	It is enough that this person has been punished in this way by most of you.

this punishment by the majority: or "the punishment imposed by the
majority." We don't know what the punishment was, but this makes it
clear that Paul and his readers knew. Instead of the majority (TEV
"most of you"), the meaning of the Greek may be "the group" or "the
congregation."
is enough: that is, it was adequate, it was fair and just. Whatever
the punishment was, the offender deserved it; it wasn't too much. But
it should not go beyond what was fair.

2.7 RSV	TEV
so you should rather turn to for-give and comfort him, or he may be overwhelmed by excessive sorrow.	Now, however, you should forgive him and encourage him, in order to keep him from becoming so sad as to give up completely.

turn to forgive and comfort him: by turn RSV presumably means "to
change," "to act differently."
forgive: in the context of human relationships forgiveness involves
a willingness to forget what has been done and to treat the offender as
though he or she had not committed a wrong. In the context of the
Christian church it means to welcome such a person back into the full
fellowship of the community of faith.
comfort: see 1.3-4. Here the sense is "encourage" (TEV) or "reassure."
or he may be: "so that he will not be," "to keep him from being."
overwhelmed by excessive sorrow: the Greek verb means "be swallowed," "be drowned." Here the sorrow may well be remorse; probably it
is the pain and sorrow of being excluded from the Christian fellowship.

2.8 RSV	TEV
So I beg you to reaffirm your love for him.	And so I beg you to let him know that you really do love him.

reaffirm your love for him: "tell him that you really do love him,"
"reassure him of your love for him." Some take the verb translated reaffirm to include a formal action; this may be so, and some translations have, "I beg you to give him some definite proof of your love
for him."

2.9 RSV	TEV
For this is why I wrote, that I might test you and know whether you are obedient in everything.	I wrote you that letter because I wanted to find out how well you had stood the test and whether you are always ready to obey my instructions.

For: there is no causal relationship between this verse and the preceding verse, and so it is better to begin the verse as TEV does.

I wrote: this is the letter referred to in verses 3-4; consequently, TEV has "I wrote you that letter."

I might test you: Paul wanted to find out if the Corinthian Christians would follow his instructions with regard to the offending person. This is the meaning of RSV. But the Greek word may be taken to mean "result of a test," and this is how TEV and others translate. In this sense, the purpose of the letter was to find out how well the Corinthian Christians had come through the difficult experience. Some translate "to prove your loyalty (to me)."

you are obedient in everything: that is, to Paul; so TEV "you are always ready to obey my instructions."

The verse may be translated as follows:

I wrote that letter in order to test you and find out if you are always ready to obey me.

Implicit in the statement is Paul's belief that the Corinthian Christians had proved themselves loyal and were always ready to follow his instructions.

2.10 RSV	TEV
Any one whom you forgive, I also forgive. What I have forgiven, if I have forgiven anything, has been for your sake in the presence of Christ,	When you forgive someone for what he has done, I forgive him too. For when I forgive—if, indeed, I need to forgive anything—I do it in Christ's presence because of you,

Paul wishes them to know that he is satisfied, and that if they forgive the offender he is ready to do the same: "So if you will forgive someone, I also will forgive him."

if I have forgiven anything: again, with the utmost tact Paul tries to bring about a reconciliation with the offender. What he is saying is in the way of a concession: "if, in fact, there is anything I need to forgive."

for your sake: "for your benefit," that is, "because I care for you."

in the presence of Christ: "with Christ as my witness." Paul is stressing the nature of forgiveness as a free and sincere action, performed in the presence, as it were, of the Christ who forgives us. The translation may have to say "as though Christ were present," "knowing that Christ sees what I do," "with Christ as my witness."

2.11   RSV   TEV

RSV	TEV
to keep Satan from gaining the advantage over us; for we are not ignorant of his designs.	in order to keep Satan from getting the upper hand over us; for we know what his plans are.

to keep: since this makes the sentence quite long and complex, it may be better to end verse 10 with a full stop and begin verse 11: "And so we keep..." or "For in this way Satan does not...." Or else, "I do this so that Satan...."

Satan is the Devil, the ruler of the forces of evil; the name Satan means "the opponent."

gaining the advantage over us: the idea Paul is expressing is that by forgiving the offender and assuring him of their love, the Corinthian Christians will keep themselves safe from evil—Satan will not be able to control them but will be defeated. Here us is the whole Christian body. The translation can say "I do this so that Satan will not be able to have power over us."

Instead of the double negative for we are not ignorant of, TEV has the affirmative form "for we know."

designs: "plans" (TEV), "intentions," "methods."

SECTION HEADING

Paul's Anxiety in Troas: "Paul's Short Stay in Troas."

In these two verses Paul goes on telling what happened. He went to Troas hoping that there he would meet Titus, who would be returning from Corinth. Paul hoped that Titus would be bringing good news about the situation in the church there. Only at 7.5 does Paul take up the story once more of his activities after leaving Troas.

2.12   RSV   TEV

RSV	TEV
When I came to Troas to preach the gospel of Christ, a door was opened for me in the Lord;	When I arrived in Troas to preach the Good News about Christ, I found that the Lord had opened the way for the work there.

Troas was a port city on the Aegean Sea, in the western part of the Roman province of Asia. Paul had left Ephesus and gone to Troas; and from there he went on to the province of Macedonia.

to preach the gospel of Christ: "to proclaim the Good News about Christ."

a door was opened for me in the Lord: the literal translation of the Greek makes no sense in English. The figure of "an open door" stands for opportunity. The phrase in the Lord means that the Lord provided the opportunity for Paul to proclaim the Good News. Here the Lord may be God but probably is the Lord Jesus Christ.

The translation can follow TEV: "I found that the Lord had opened the way for the work there" or "...for me to work there." Or else,

"the Lord provided me an excellent opportunity to do my work there" or
"...to preach the gospel there."

2.13	RSV	TEV
	but my mind could not rest because I did not find my brother Titus there. So I took leave of them and went on to Macedonia.	But I was deeply worried, because I could not find our brother Titus. So I said good-bye to the people there and went on to Macedonia.

It is better to make a complete stop at the end of verse 12, as in
TEV, and begin a new sentence at verse 13.
my mind could not rest: "I was deeply worried" (TEV), "I was very
upset."
my brother: the Greek has the first person singular my; but as
this may lead the readers to understand that Titus was a blood brother
of Paul, it is better to say "our brother" (TEV) as in 1.1. Titus was
a companion and helper of Paul (see Gal 2.1-3).
I took leave of them: "I said good-bye to the people there" (TEV),
"I said farewell to our Christian brothers and sisters in Troas."
Macedonia: see 1.16.

SECTION HEADING

Victory through Christ: "Christ Gives Us the Victory," "The Apostles Share Christ's Victory."

Beginning here, and going through 7.4, Paul talks about the work
of the apostles, that is, those who proclaim the Good News. He describes
the joy and the pain, the happiness and the sadness, the successes and
the failures, that this ministry brings.
In this short section Paul bursts into a prayer of praise, and
defends his own work as an apostle.

2.14	RSV	TEV
	But thanks be to God, who in Christ always leads us in triumph, and through us spreads the fragrance of the knowledge of him everywhere.	But thanks be to God! For in union with Christ we are always led by God as prisoners in Christ's victory procession. God uses us to make the knowledge about Christ spread everywhere like a sweet fragrance.

thanks be to God: "let us praise (or, thank) God."
in Christ: this phrase, and the similar "in the Lord," are employed
by Paul very often to refer to the Christian life as union with Christ
Jesus. In some contexts the phrase means "as a Christian" or "the Christian life (or, way)." Here it means "our life in union with Christ."
leads us in triumph: the us refers to Paul and his companions or,
in a more general way, to all who proclaim the gospel. The latter seems

preferable. The Greek word translated triumph means more precisely "triumphal parade," "victory procession." When Roman generals returned to Rome after successful military campaigns, sometimes they and their soldiers had a victory procession through the streets of Rome. Captured enemies would be forced to march in the procession. Here Paul pictures himself and his fellow apostles as captives who accompany the victory procession of Christ; so TEV "in union with Christ we are always led by God as prisoners in Christ's victory procession." Some take the Greek to mean simply "we share in Christ's victory procession," not as prisoners but as allies, or soldiers, of the victorious Christ. So the translation could be "But thanks be to God! For he always leads us in Christ's victory procession" or, in more general terms, "...For he always causes us to share in Christ's victory." In languages where the idea of a victory procession is difficult if not impossible to portray, the general idea of sharing in Christ's victory over the powers of evil may be expressed as follows: "God has made Christ victorious over the power of evil (or, sin), and we apostles share in Christ's victory."

In another figure, the fragrance of the knowledge of him, Paul compares the gospel message, that is, "the knowledge about Christ" (TEV), to the pleasant aroma of incense. The burning of incense was part of the triumphal parade of the victorious general, and Paul seems to be alluding to it here. TEV translates "God uses us to make the knowledge about Christ spread everywhere like a sweet fragrance"; another way of translating would be "God uses us to proclaim the message about Christ; it is like a pleasant smell that spreads everywhere." If the idea of fragrance, or a pleasing smell, is difficult, a more general statement can be made: "God uses us to make the message about Christ known everywhere" or "...to spread the message about Christ everywhere."

2.15	RSV	TEV
	For we are the aroma of Christ to God among those who are being saved and among those who are perishing,	For we are like a sweet-smelling incense offered by Christ to God, which spreads among those who are being saved and those who are being lost.

Paul continues the figure of incense: we are the aroma of Christ. The meaning is not, as the RSV literal translation says, that the apostles are Christ's odor; here the word refers to incense, a sweet-smelling substance burned in religious services. Instead of the metaphor "We are the incense that Christ offers to God," a simile may be better: "For we are like a sweet-smelling incense offered by Christ to God" (TEV), or "...a sweet-smelling incense that Christ burns as an offering to God."

But the figure of incense may not be appropriate in a given language, and so another way of representing the statement may be required. In connection with the rest of the verse, among those who are being saved and among those who are perishing, the meaning is that the gospel, the message proclaimed by the apostles, is spread among all people. If the figure of sweet-smelling incense is retained, the verse may be translated as TEV has done. But if the figure is not retained, the verse may

[27]

be translated as follows: "For it is through us that the Good News about Christ is proclaimed to all people, to those who are being saved and to those who are being lost."

The idea of "being saved" and "being lost" may have to be expressed in a different way: "those who are on the way that leads to eternal life" and "those who are on the road to eternal death."

2.16	RSV	TEV
	to one a fragrance from death to death, to the other a fragrance from life to life. Who is sufficient for these things?	For those who are being lost, it is a deadly stench that kills; but for those who are being saved, it is a fragrance that brings life. Who, then, is capable for such a task?

Paul continues with the aroma of incense as a figure of the Christian message. The Christian message promises life and salvation to those who accept Christ, but death and destruction for those who reject him. It is a message both of salvation and of condemnation. A person determines the consequence of the message either by accepting or rejecting Christ.

from death to death...from life to life: emphatic ways of describing the result: "a deadly stench that kills...a fragrance that brings life" (TEV).

Again, if the figure of an aroma is impossible to carry over in translation, the translation here can be: "For those who are being lost, the Christian message means death; for those who are being saved, it means life." The language "being lost" and "being saved" does not state who is responsible; it simply portrays the condition as a continuing event, a process, and not an act.

The question Who is sufficient for these things? has to do with the apostolic task of proclaiming the Good News. The knowledge that the proclamation of the gospel results in life for some and death for others causes Paul to exclaim "Who, then, is capable for such a task?" (TEV). Or, "Who has the capacity to do this work?" or "Who is qualified for such an important task?" The question is not completely rhetorical, that is, it is not Paul's way of saying that no one is capable, since in the next verse he implicitly affirms that he and his companions are capable (see also 3.5-6). Apart from Christ's power and authority, however, no person is qualified for this task.

2.17	RSV	TEV
	For we are not, like so many, peddlers of God's word; but as men of sincerity, as commissioned by God, in the sight of God we speak in Christ.	We are not like so many others, who handle God's message as if it were cheap merchandise; but because God has sent us, we speak with sincerity in his presence, as servants of Christ.

we are not, like so many, peddlers of God's word: here Paul implicitly answers the question of verse 16: "We are capable for this task,
because we are not...." Here we refers to Paul and his companions.

Paul contrasts himself and his companions with many (TEV "many
others"), and he says that those others are like peddlers of the gospel.
The Greek verb describes people who handle the Christian message as
though it were merchandise, as though it were a product which they sell
in order to make a living. Paul does not identify the people he says
are like peddlers of the gospel.

God's word: the gospel; "the message from God," "the Good News."

commissioned by God: "given this task by God," or "sent by God"
(see TEV).

in the sight of God: as in the presence of Christ in 2.10, the
idea here is that God is a witness to what the apostles do; the translation can say "God himself knows," "God sees."

we speak in Christ: TEV "we speak...as servants of Christ." Here
in Christ can be taken to mean "in union with Christ" (see 2.14). Or
else, "as messengers of Christ."

The verse may be translated as follows:
We are not like many others, who are not qualified for this
work. They proclaim the gospel as though it were only a
business from which to earn a living. But we are honest
and sincere in our work; we proclaim the gospel under God's
direction, as messengers sent by him and as servants of
Christ.

Chapter 3

Servants of the New Covenant: "The New Covenant," "The Covenant from God's Spirit."

In this chapter Paul writes about the new covenant, of which the Christian apostles are servants, as compared with the old covenant, the one given through Moses. In all respects the new one is better than the old one.

3.1 RSV	TEV
Are we beginning to commend ourselves again? Or do we need, as some do, letters of recommendation to you, or from you?	Does this sound as if we were again boasting about ourselves? Could it be that, like some other people, we need letters of recommendation to you or from you?

Paul begins with a question which seems to imply that he and his companions had been accused of bragging about themselves: Are we beginning to commend ourselves again? The statement in the preceding verse (2.17) about how he and his companions proclaimed the gospel in a sincere way sounds like boasting—and Paul is sensitive to the criticism. The question is a way of saying "In saying this we are not boasting about ourselves again."

do we need...letters of recommendation...?: these are letters that churches would give Christian messengers as they went to other churches, letters to introduce the messengers (see Acts 18.27). The form of the question in Greek makes it clear that Paul means to say 'We don't need letters of recommendation....'"

letters of recommendation: "letters that introduce us," "letters that tell others that we are really Christian messengers," "letters that show that we have the approval of the churches."

as some do: obviously anyone who was not well known would need such a letter. Paul and his companions are known and welcomed by all churches, and do not need letters.

The verse may be translated as follows:

What I have just written does not mean, as some would say, that we are bragging about ourselves again. We are not like other people; we don't need letters that recommend us to you. Nor do we need to ask you to write letters that recommend us to others.

There is a wordplay in Greek that RSV represents by commend and recommendation. If the language level allows it, something like the following could be said:

> Does this sound like we are recommending ourselves
> again? No! We don't need letters of recommendation, as
> some people do. We don't need letters from others to
> recommend us to you, or letters from you recommending
> us to others.

3.2 RSV	TEV
You yourselves are our letter of recommendation, written on your^c hearts, to be known and read by all men;	You yourselves are the letter we have, written on our hearts for everyone to know and read.

^{c}Other ancient authorities read
our

You yourselves are our letter of recommendation: Paul applies the
figure of a letter of recommendation to the Corinthian Christians: they
themselves are all the recommendation that Paul and his companions need.
Their work at Corinth was proof of the fact that they were genuine
apostles.

It may be necessary to use a simile: "You yourselves are like a
letter of recommendation for us."

written on your hearts: RSV follows a Greek text that has your,
which takes the "letter of recommendation" from Corinth to be the deep
love and concern of the Corinthian Christians for Paul and his colleagues. But the manuscript support for "our hearts" (TEV) is stronger
and fits better in the context. What Paul had accomplished in Corinth,
and his deep love for the Corinthian Christians, are kept in his heart,
and everyone knows that this is so. Paul and his companions need no
other letter of recommendation.

by all men: "by all people." Or, "for everyone to know and read"
(TEV); or else, "for everyone to read and understand."

3.3 RSV	TEV
and you show that you are a letter from Christ delivered by us, writ- ten not with ink but with the Spirit of the living God, not on tablets of stone but on tablets of human hearts.	It is clear that Christ himself wrote this letter and sent it by us. It is written, not with ink but with the Spirit of the living God, and not on stone tablets but on human hearts.

Here Paul expands on the figure in order to make clear that the
final recommendation is from Christ, not from people.

you show: this seems to say that somehow the Corinthian Christians
were actively demonstrating that they were a letter. But it seems better to understand the Greek participle in an impersonal fashion: "It
is clear" (TEV); or, "But as for you, it is plain that..." or "...it
is evident that...."

you are a letter from Christ: "you are a letter that Christ wrote."
The final proof of genuineness comes from Christ, not from the Corinthian Christians, and the "letter" that the apostles have written on
their hearts is one that Christ himself "wrote." It may be necessary to
use a simile, "you are like a letter," instead of the metaphor you are
a letter. See the proposed translation below.

delivered by us: Paul and his companions delivered the letter that
Christ wrote, that is, made its contents known to believers everywhere.
Or else the Greek participle translated delivered (TEV "sent") may mean
"written"—that is, the "letter" which the Corinthian Christians were
had Christ as the author, and Paul as the actual writer to whom Christ
dictated the "letter." The metaphor is not too clear; what Paul is anxious to show is that the basis of his apostolic authority is from Christ,
and that the Corinthian Christians are evidence of this. Paul had been
Christ's instrument in their conversion to the Christian faith.

written: what follows supports the interpretation that Paul (and
his companions) delivered the letter, not that they wrote it. Christ
himself is the writer of the letter.

The contrasts not with ink but with the Spirit of the living God
and not on tablets of stone but on tablets of human hearts are made in
order to show the divine and spiritual nature of the "letter" that the
Corinthian Christians are. It may be impossible to preserve the figure
written...with the Spirit of the living God...on tablets of human
hearts. If so, the best thing is to change the metaphor to a simile:

You are like a letter that Christ wrote and sent by us.
This is not a letter that someone writes with ink on stone
tablets. Instead, this is, as it were, a letter that Christ,
by means of the Spirit of the living God, wrote on human
hearts.

If the metaphor is retained, TEV may be followed.

	3.4 RSV	TEV

3.4   RSV — Such is the confidence that we have through Christ toward God.

TEV — We say this because we have confidence in God through Christ.

Such is the confidence: it is better to translate as TEV has done:
"We say this because we have confidence." This connects the verse more
clearly with the preceding verse. This confidence is Paul's assurance
that the Corinthian Christians are all the evidence he needs to prove
that he is a true apostle. It is based on God's call and is given
through Christ.

The verse may be translated as follows: "It is because of our
confidence in God, which Christ gives us, that we can say these things."

3.5   RSV — Not that we are competent of ourselves to claim anything as coming
from us; our competence is from
God,

TEV — There is nothing in us that allows
us to claim that we are capable of
doing this work. The capacity we
have comes from God;

competent: "fit," "capable" (TEV), "adequate for." This refers
back to 2.16.

to claim anything as coming from us: "to claim that any ability
we have (for our work) is our own." Paul is saying that whatever capacity he and his companions have is God's gift, not their own achievement.
TEV may be followed; or else, "We ourselves have nothing in us that
gives us the right to claim that we are capable of doing this work."

our competence is from God: "it is God who makes us competent";
"The capacity we have comes from God" (TEV); "it is God who gives us
the capacity (for the work)."

3.6 RSV	TEV
who has made us competent to be ministers of a new covenant, not in a written code but in the Spirit; for the written code kills, but the Spirit gives life.	it is he who made us capable of serving the new covenant, which consists not of a written law but of the Spirit. The written law brings death, but the Spirit gives life.

ministers of a new covenant: here ministers means "servants," not
ordained clerics. The basic idea of covenant in the Bible is not a
contract, where two parties meet as equals and work out the terms for
an agreement between them; rather it is God's plan for his people which
he, in grace and love, offers them for their good. He promises to bless
them and protect them if they acknowledge and obey him as their God.
At Mount Sinai God offered his covenant, through Moses, to the people
of Israel, and they accepted what God offered (Exo 24.8). Jeremiah
31.31-34 spoke of the new covenant which God would give his people,
and the promise came true in Christ (1 Cor 11.25; Heb 12.24). It may
not be possible or natural to speak of being servants of a covenant,
so it may be necessary to say "serving God in the way provided for by
a new covenant."

not in a written code but in the Spirit: it is better, with TEV,
to make a relative clause, "which consists not of...," or else to begin
a new sentence, "This new covenant is not a written law...." Another
possibility is to say "In this new covenant we do not obey a written
law but the Spirit (of God)." This written code is an obvious reference
to the Sinai covenant, which was given in the form of the Law, the
commandments.

The new covenant consists of the Spirit; that is, under the terms
of the new covenant the people of God are not directed by a written
Law but by God's Spirit.

the written code kills: or "The written law brings death" (TEV).
The Law of Moses required the people to act in certain ways, but was
unable itself to give them the moral strength and wisdom to follow
these commands. The result could only be death, that is, spiritual
death. But the Spirit of God gives people spiritual life.

3.7-8 RSV	TEV
Now if the dispensation of death, carved in letters on stone, came with such splendor that the Israelites could not look at Moses' face because of its brightness, fading as this was, 8 will not the dispensation of the Spirit be attended with greater splendor?	The Law was carved in letters on stone tablets, and God's glory appeared when it was given. Even though the brightness on Moses' face was fading, it was so strong that the people of Israel could not keep their eyes fixed on him. If the Law, which brings death when it is in force, came with such glory, 8 how much greater is the glory that belongs to the activity of the Spirit!

As RSV shows, these two verses in Greek form one long complex sentence. It is better to break the text up into two or more sentences. The RSV formal equivalence does not qualify as an acceptable translation, since it is impossible to understand.

the dispensation of death: this refers to the giving of the Law to Moses at Mount Sinai, and contrasts with the dispensation of the Spirit in verse 8. Linguistically RSV reproduces the parallelism of the Greek text, but makes no sense in English. Paul is contrasting two covenants, the Hebrew covenant and the Christian covenant. The old one, as already said in verse 6, brings death; the new one, the covenant of the Spirit, brings life.

It is better, as TEV has done, to describe the circumstances surrounding the giving of the Hebrew covenant at Mount Sinai, and then, as a question (RSV) or as a statement (TEV), contrast the old with the new.

the dispensation of death...came with such splendor: "when the Law, which condemns to death (or, which results in spiritual death), ...was given, God's glory appeared." This splendor is the glory of God, the bright light which appeared on Mount Sinai when the Law was given (see Exo 24.16-17; 33.18-23). This bright light is the visible sign of God's presence.

carved in letters on stone: or "carved, letter by letter, on stone." The Law was engraved on two stone tablets (Exo 31.18; 32.16; 34.28).

such splendor...Moses' face because of its brightness: this refers to the account that when Moses came down from Mount Sinai to the people, his face was shining because he had been in the presence of God (Exo 34.29-35).

fading as this was: here Paul describes the shining on Moses' face as a temporary phenomenon (see verse 13, below).

the dispensation of the Spirit: the new covenant is the covenant of the Spirit, that is, it operates by the power of God's Spirit in the lives of God's people.

will not the dispensation of the Spirit be attended with greater splendor?: the form of the question implies that the dispensation of the Spirit is a future event. But the form of the verb will is required by the conditional statement, Now if the dispensation of death...came. In relation to the giving of the Law of Moses, the new covenant was a future event; but it had already been inaugurated by Jesus Christ when Paul wrote this letter. It is better, therefore, not to use a rhetorical question, as RSV does, but to translate as a statement: "how much greater is the glory that belongs to the activity of the Spirit!" (TEV); or, "when the new covenant, the covenant of the Spirit, began, there was a much greater manifestation of God's glory.

Verses 7-8 may be translated as follows:

> The written Law was carved on stone tablets, and when it was given, God's glory (or, God's shining brightness) appeared. The face of Moses shone with that glory, and even though it was fading away, it was so strong that the people of Israel could not keep looking at Moses' face. God's glory (or, brightness), then, appeared when the Law, which brings death, was given. But the glory when the covenant of the Spirit was inaugurated (or, was given) was much greater.

3.9	RSV	TEV
	For if there was splendor in the dispensation of condemnation, the dispensation of righteousness must far exceed it in splendor.	The system which brings condemnation was glorious; how much more glorious is the activity which brings salvation!

Paul now compares the two by calling the Law of Moses the dispensation of condemnation and the gospel the dispensation of righteousness. Here condemnation says the same thing that kills says in verse 6: it is the condemnation to punishment and death. Its opposite is called righteousness, which here is used in the sense in which the equivalent Hebrew word is often used in the Old Testament: "salvation" (TEV), "acquittal," "forgiveness," or even "(spiritual) life." Or else the two may be contrasted: "being condemned by God...being put into the right relationship with God" (see Rom 1.17).

RSV uses the word dispensation twice, reflecting the Greek, which uses the same word twice. TEV has "The system" and "the activity." Other possible ways of translating this would be "For if the Law, which brings condemnation...the gospel, which brings salvation"; or "the old covenant...the new covenant"; or "the giving of the Law...the giving of the Spirit." Throughout this passage Paul uses different sets of terms to speak about the same two crucial events, the giving of the Law of Moses in the old covenant, and the giving of the gospel in the new covenant.

3.10	RSV	TEV
	Indeed, in this case, what once had splendor has come to have no splendor at all, because of the splendor that surpasses it.	We may say that because of the far brighter glory now the glory that was so bright in the past is gone.

Paul now contrasts the degree of splendor or "glory" (TEV) in the two covenants. From the initial meaning of the shining brightness of God's presence, the word now becomes a figure for the value, or importance, of each covenant, or else the degree to which each reveals God's nature. The Law is no longer glorious because the gospel is so much more glorious. Some commentators use the figure of a lit candle, which in the bright sunlight seems to give no light at all because of the stronger light given by the sun.

3.11   RSV   TEV
For if what faded away came with   For if there was glory in that
splendor, what is permanent must   which lasted for a while, how much
have much more splendor.   more glory is there in that which
                                       lasts forever!

Paul makes the same point again, contrasting the two, this time in terms of permanence: the former system, the Law, was temporary; the present system, the gospel, is permanent.

Instead of the conditional form, used both in RSV and TEV, a statement may be better: "That which was temporary had glory; that which is permanent has much more glory!" Or, "The old covenant, which was only for a while, was splendid; the new covenant, which is eternal, is much more splendid."

3.12   RSV   TEV
Since we have such a hope, we   Because we have this hope, we
are very bold,   are very bold.

hope: see 1.7. Here also, the meaning is "confidence," "assurance" (3.1).

we are very bold: "we speak boldly," "we speak with assurance." Paul and his companions have confidence in the gospel of which they are servants. They believe it is the work of God's Spirit, that it is eternal, and that it brings spiritual life. Because of this, Paul and his companions are bold in proclaiming the gospel.

3.13   RSV   TEV
not like Moses, who put a veil   We are not like Moses, who had to
over his face so that the Israel-   put a veil over his face so that
ites might not see the end of the   the people of Israel would not see
fading splendor.   the brightness fade and disappear.

Here Paul refers to the veil which Moses put over his face (see Exo 34.29-35). He explains it as an attempt to keep the people of Israel from seeing that the brightness was fading from Moses' face. Paul is saying that the apostles proclaim a message which is forever true and valid; it will never become irrelevant or disappear. So Paul and his companions always boldly proclaim the Good News.

see the end of the fading splendor: "see the brightness fade and disappear" (TEV); or "see that the brightness was fading away."

3.14   RSV   TEV

But their minds were hardened; for   Their minds, indeed, were closed;
to this day, when they read the old   and to this very day their minds
covenant, that same veil remains   are covered with the same veil as
unlifted, because only through   they read the books of the old
Christ is it taken away.   covenant. The veil is removed only
                                       when a person is joined to Christ.

their minds were hardened: "they were unable to understand," "they
had lost their capacity of understanding."
    Here the effect of the veil is described in terms of the people of
Israel; Paul says they were and are unable to understand, if not unwilling to understand. In saying "Their minds, indeed, were closed" (TEV),
Paul is referring to the people of Israel in the time of Moses. But
then Paul says that the same condition is true in his own time: "to
this very day their minds are covered with the same veil" (TEV).
    that same veil remains unlifted: here the veil is thought of as
transferred from Moses to the people of Israel.
    they read the old covenant: that is, "they read the books of the
old covenant" (TEV), the Old Testament Scriptures. Or, "when the books
of the old covenant are read to them," that is, in the synagogue services.
    It is only through Christ that the veil is removed, that is, that
the Israelites (and all others) can understand what the Law and the
gospel really mean. The phrase through Christ translates the Greek "in
Christ" (see 2.14). TEV translates "joined to Christ"; or "when a person becomes a Christian." Or the translation could be "the veil is removed by Christ."

3.15-16   RSV   TEV

Yes, to this day whenever Moses is   Even today, whenever they read
read a veil lies over their minds;   the Law of Moses, the veil still
16 but when a man turns to the   covers their minds. 16 But it can
Lord the veil is removed.   be removed, as the scripture says
                                       about Moses: "His veil was removed
                                       when he turned to the Lord."*c*

                                       cVerse 16 may be translated: But
                                       the veil is removed whenever
                                       someone turns to the Lord.

    As translated by RSV, these two verses say exactly the same thing
said in verse 14. Verse 15 quite clearly repeats what is said in the
middle of verse 14.
    whenever Moses is read: that is, "whenever the Law of Moses is
read (or, the books of Moses are read)" in the synagogue. TEV and others
translate "whenever they read the Law of Moses." Here Moses means the
same as the old covenant in verse 14, that is, the Hebrew Scriptures.
    RSV takes verse 16 to mean the same that is said in the last part
of verse 14: when a man turns to the Lord the veil is removed. This
should be "whenever a person turns to the Lord" (see alternate

translation in TEV footnote). Here <u>the Lord</u> is Jesus Christ. But there is another possible interpretation of verse 16, found in TEV and other translations. These translations take "when (or, whenever) he turns to the Lord" to refer to Moses, as reported in Exodus 34.34: "Whenever Moses went into the Tent of the Lord's presence to speak to the Lord, he would take the veil off." In the Old Testament passage "the Lord" refers to God.

There is no way of deciding which meaning is more likely; most translations are like RSV.

3.17   RSV

Now the Lord is the Spirit, and where the Spirit of the Lord is, there is freedom.

TEV

Now, "the Lord" in this passage is the Spirit; and where the Spirit of the Lord is present, there is freedom.

<u>the Lord is the Spirit</u>: in the RSV translation of verse 16, <u>the Lord</u> is Jesus Christ, that is, the risen and glorified Christ. Here in verse 17, then, the meaning is the same. TEV, however, takes verse 16 to be a reference to Moses and understands the statement here in verse 17 to be Paul's interpretation of the title "the LORD" (in Exo 34.34): "Now, 'the Lord' in this passage is the Spirit." Or else, "In this passage, the title 'the Lord' refers to the Spirit (or, to God's Spirit)."

<u>where the Spirit of the Lord is, there is freedom</u>: "whoever has the Spirit of the Lord (or, is guided by the Spirit of the Lord) is free." The freedom Paul speaks of is spiritual freedom, freedom from the Law, and from sin and death.

3.18   RSV

And we all, with unveiled face, beholding[d] the glory of the Lord, are being changed into his likeness from one degree of glory to another; for this comes from the Lord who is the Spirit.

TEV

All of us, then, reflect the glory of the Lord with uncovered faces; and that same glory, coming from the Lord, who is the Spirit, transforms us into his likeness in an ever greater degree of glory.

[d]Or *reflecting*

<u>we all</u>: all Christians.

<u>with unveiled faces</u>: "with no veil over our faces," "with our faces uncovered."

<u>beholding the glory of the Lord</u>: "seeing the glory of the Lord." "We all, with no covering (or, veil) on our faces, see the glory of the Lord." Or, "We do not have a veil over our faces, and so we see the glory of the Lord." TEV (see RSV footnote) interprets the Greek verb to mean "reflecting": "All of us, then, reflect the glory of the Lord...." The Greek verb means "to reflect as a mirror," and some translations have "we reflect like a mirror the glory of the Lord." Here again, <u>glory</u> is a shining brightness, but the word is now used in a figurative way. Paul is not talking about a light but about the nature of God.

are being changed into his likeness: "are continually being made
more and more like him." Christians not only reflect the glory of the
risen Lord, but they are also changed by it. The Greek verb translated
changed is the verb used in Mark 9.2 of the change that came over Jesus
on the mountain.

from one degree of glory to another: that is, "an ever greater degree of glory" (TEV), or "...intensity of glory."

this comes from the Lord: the whole process of change is caused
by the Lord.

Instead of the passive form of the Greek ("we are being transformed"), TEV has used an active construction, "and that same glory...
transforms us into his likeness in an ever greater degree of glory."
This could be said otherwise: "and that glory, which comes (or, shines)
from the Lord, who is the Spirit, keeps on changing us. We become ever
more like him, and have more and more of his glory."

the Lord who is the Spirit: or, better, "the Lord, who is the
Spirit." Some translations have "the Spirit of the Lord"; this is possible but is not very probable.

Chapter 4

Spiritual Treasure in Clay Pots: "Human Weakness and God's Power," "Defeat and Victory."

Paul continues talking about his work as an apostle. Throughout this section he uses the first person plural, which indicates that he is speaking of himself and his companions. But it may be that Paul is speaking only of himself, and some translations use the first person singular. It seems better, however, to retain the plural form.

Some make a separate section of verses 1-6, with the heading "Light and Darkness" or "God's Light Shines in the Darkness." Most translations divide the text as TEV does.

Paul speaks realistically and eloquently of the task of proclaiming the gospel, the difficulties that must be faced, and the suffering that must be endured. But above all Paul speaks of the grace and power of God, which sustains the apostles and assures them of victory.

4.1	RSV	TEV
	Therefore, having this ministry by the mercy of God,^{e} we do not lose heart.	God in his mercy has given us this work to do, and so we do not become discouraged.

^{e}Greek *as we have received mercy*

Therefore: logically this goes with the last part of the verse; so TEV has "and so we do not...."

having this ministry by the mercy of God: "because of his mercy, God has given us this task," "God is merciful, and so he has given us this work (of proclaiming the gospel)." Here mercy is God's goodness, his kindly attitude toward human beings in general, and more explicitly here, toward Paul and his companions. "Because God is good, he has given us this work to do."

we do not lose heart: "we do not become discouraged" (TEV), "we don't give up."

The verse may be translated as follows:
So we do not become discouraged, for we know that it is because of God's goodness that he has given us this task to perform.

4.2 RSV	TEV
We have renounced disgraceful, underhanded ways; we refuse to practice cunning or to tamper with God's word, but by the open statement of the truth we would commend ourselves to every man's conscience in the sight of God.	We put aside all secret and shameful deeds; we do not act with deceit, nor do we falsify the word of God. In the full light of truth we live in God's sight and try to commend ourselves to everyone's good conscience.

We have renounced disgraceful, underhanded ways: this seems to imply that there were people who acted in this way (see 2.17).

renounced: this word in RSV suggests the wrong idea, that Paul once did these things but no longer does them. And so it is better to say "put aside" (TEV), "reject," "abstain from"; or "We do not use," "We have nothing to do with."

disgraceful, underhanded ways: "secret and shameful deeds" (TEV), "shameful things done in secret." Paul does not explain what these deeds are; perhaps he is referring to what follows.

we refuse to practice cunning: or "we do not act with deceit" (TEV); "we do not try to deceive people."

we refuse...to tamper with God's word: the Greek verb means "to falsify" (TEV), "to adulterate," "to distort," "to change" (that is, in a bad way).

God's word has here the same meaning it does in 2.17: the Christian message proclaimed by the apostles.

by the open statement of the truth: "we speak only the truth," "declaring the truth openly," "bringing the truth to light." TEV "In the full light of truth" takes the Greek noun for "manifestation" in an abstract way, meaning the setting in which Paul and his companions proclaim the gospel. But it seems better to take the word in the active sense of Paul's proclamation, and so "we speak the truth openly," "we openly declare the truth." In this context the truth is the gospel message, the truth about God and his will for humankind.

commend ourselves: as in 3.1.

we would commend ourselves to every man's conscience: "we try to make a good impression on everyone," "we want people to have a good opinion of us." This does not mean that Paul would be deceitful or hypocritical; rather, Paul hopes that people will see that he acts with integrity and sincerity, and that they will approve of him. He was doing nothing that should cause others to disapprove of him and his companions. The last part of the verse may be translated as follows: "With God as our witness, we openly declare the truth of the gospel. By doing this, we hope that everyone will have a good opinion of us (or, approve of what we are doing)." For conscience see 1.12; here it means a person's judgment or opinion.

in the sight of God: see the similar phrase in 2.17. Here the phrase modifies the apostles' action, we would commend ourselves, and not every man's conscience (see TEV).

4.3 RSV	TEV
And even if our gospel is veiled, it is veiled only to those who are perishing.	For if the gospel we preach is hidden, it is hidden only from those who are being lost.

our gospel: "the message (of salvation) that we proclaim," "the Good News we proclaim." Here our refers to Paul and his co-workers.

is veiled: this refers back to 3.14-15. Here also it means that people are unwilling or unable to understand the gospel message. TEV "hidden" means "obscure," "difficult (or, impossible) to understand." The conditional form if our gospel is veiled is a way of making an affirmative statement, with the explanation following in verse 4: "The message that we proclaim may be difficult to understand, but...," or "Although the message we proclaim is impossible to understand, it is so only in the case of those who...," or "Some people find our message impossible to understand; but it is only those who...," or "Some people, as a matter of fact, do not understand the message we proclaim, but these are the people who are being lost."

those who are perishing: see 2.15.

4.4 RSV	TEV
In their case the god of this world has blinded the minds of the unbelievers, to keep them from seeing the light of the gospel of the glory of Christ, who is the likeness of God.	They do not believe, because their minds have been kept in the dark by the evil god of this world. He keeps them from seeing the light shining on them, the light that comes from the Good News about the glory of Christ, who is the exact likeness of God.

In their case...the unbelievers: RSV makes it appear that these are two different groups: (1) those who are perishing (verse 3, to whom In their case refers) and (2) the unbelievers. Of course these are the same people. TEV makes this clear by beginning verse 4: "They do not believe...." It may be necessary to say explicitly "They do not believe our message," "They refuse to believe the gospel."

the god of this world: this is a reference to Satan (2.11). It may be necessary to say, like TEV, "the evil god of this world," or else, "Satan, who is the god of (or, the god who rules over) this world." Paul's language should be respected, and the translation should make it clear that he is speaking of Satan as the ruler of the world.

blinded the minds: "made them unable to understand." The figure describes lack of perception, lack of rational thinking. Satan kept them from thinking straight, and so they did not accept the gospel message.

to keep them from seeing: this is the effect of the blinding of their minds. It is not only a matter of intellectual understanding, but of spiritual insight.

the light of the gospel: "the light shining on them, the light that comes from the Good News" (TEV). TEV translates in this way because the Greek word means not only "light" as such, but "illumination," that is, the shining of the light upon them.

the gospel of the glory of Christ: "the Good News about the glory of Christ" (TEV).

The glory of Christ is a way of talking about the saving presence of Christ (see 3.7-11). The shining light of God's presence appeared to the Israelites in the Old Testament as a sign that God was with them, to protect and lead them. It is now through Christ that God is present with his people.

the likeness of God: "the image of God," "the exact likeness of God" (TEV). It may be necessary to use a verbal expression, not an abstract noun. So "who is like God" or "who is of the same nature as God." Paul adds this statement in order to make clear that the saving glory of Christ is the same as the saving glory of God; there is no difference between the two. What God is, Christ also is; what God does, Christ also does.

The verse may be translated as follows:
They do not believe the gospel because Satan, the evil god of this world, has made them spiritually blind. They cannot see the light that shines on them. This is the light that is spread by the message (or, the Good News) about the glory of Christ, who is exactly like God.

4.5 RSV	TEV
For what we preach is not ourselves, but Jesus Christ as Lord, with ourselves as your servants*f* for Jesus' sake.	For it is not ourselves that we preach; we preach Jesus Christ as Lord, and ourselves as your servants for Jesus' sake.

f Or *slaves*

For what we preach: Paul had spoken about our gospel in verse 3, and in verse 4 he referred to the gospel of the glory of Christ. So he explains quite carefully the content of the message that he and his companions proclaim. "We do not preach about ourselves; we preach that Jesus Christ is Lord" (see 1.19). The verb preach does not mean to deliver a sermon in a worship service in church; it means "proclaim," "announce."

with ourselves as your servants: or "what we say about ourselves is that we are your servants" or "...that we serve you." This is spiritual service and refers to the task of proclaiming the gospel and helping the new converts in their Christian faith.

for Jesus' sake: either "because we are followers (or, servants) of Jesus" or "to honor Jesus." It is their dedication to Jesus Christ that motivates the apostles in their work.

4.6 RSV	TEV
For it is the God who said, "Let light shine out of darkness," who has shone in our hearts to give the light of the knowledge of the glory of God in the face of Christ.	The God who said, "Out of darkness the light shall shine!" is the same God who made his light shine in our hearts, to bring us the knowledge of God's glory shining in the face of Christ.

the God who said, "Let light shine out of darkness": this is a reference to the first word of creation in Genesis 1.3: "Let there be light." The third person imperative in English is often expressed by Let. Or else, as TEV has it, "out of darkness the light shall shine!"

who has shone in our hearts: "who made the light shine in our hearts." This is a way of speaking about spiritual creation. As the universe began with the creation of light, so spiritual light marks the creation of a new person, not physically but spiritually.

to give the light of the knowledge: here light is spoken of as knowledge: once again, it is spiritual knowledge, not scientific or historical.

the glory of God in the face of Christ: or "God's glory shining in the face of Christ." It would be better to say "shining from the face of Christ." Christ, so to speak, reflects the glory of God; it is Christ who reveals and brings to humankind the saving presence of God.

The verse may be translated as follows:
God commanded at creation, "Out of darkness the light shall shine." This same God also makes his (saving) light shine in our hearts. This light makes us know the glory of God, which shines from the face of Christ.

4.7	RSV	TEV
	But we have this treasure in earthen vessels, to show that the transcendent power belongs to God and not to us.	Yet we who have this spiritual treasure are like common clay pots, in order to show that the supreme power belongs to God, not to us.

this treasure: that is, the task of proclaiming the gospel. Paul says that he and his companions are no more than "clay pots" (TEV) which hold this rich treasure. Paul uses the figure in order to show that the mighty power which the gospel has comes not from the human messengers, the apostles, but from God. It may be better, like TEV, to use a comparison: "we...are like common clay pots" or "...jars made of clay." The figure does not simply apply to the human body, weak and mortal, made of the soil of the earth (Gen 2.7), but to the entire person as such. Where clay pots are considered valuable, it will be necessary to abandon the figure: "We who have this spiritual treasure are weak and ordinary, in order to show...."

to show: "to demonstrate," "to prove"; or, "so that everyone can see."

the transcendent power: "this great power." It may be necessary to identify the power explicitly, "the great power of the gospel."

belongs to God: or "comes from God."

4.8-9	RSV	TEV
	We are afflicted in every way, but not crushed; perplexed, but not driven to despair; 9 persecuted, but not forsaken; struck down, but not destroyed;	We are often troubled, but not crushed; sometimes in doubt, but never in despair; 9 there are many enemies, but we are never without a friend; and though badly hurt at times, we are not destroyed.

The Greek text of verses 7-10 is one sentence. Verses 8-9 contain four pairs of negative and positive statements, all in the form of participles, which serve to describe all these actions as things that are still happening to Paul and his companions.

We are afflicted in every way, but not crushed: the verb translated afflicted is the one used in 1.6. "We face difficulties (or, troubles) everywhere," "We are often troubled" (TEV), or "We are persecuted everywhere." It may be necessary to use active verbs: "People trouble (or, harass) us, but they cannot stop us."

not crushed: "we are not defeated," "we do not give up."

perplexed, but not driven to despair: "bewildered, but have not given up hope"; TEV "sometimes in doubt, but never in despair."

persecuted, but not forsaken: "we are persecuted by people, but never abandoned by God"; or, in the active form, "people persecute us, but God does not abandon us." TEV "there are many enemies, but we are never without a friend" is meant to be understood as referring to human enemies, and to God, the heavenly friend.

struck down, but not destroyed: "knocked down, but not killed." The language seems to refer to actual physical abuse, but it may be a way of talking about emotional and psychological anguish. TEV has "though badly hurt at times, we are not destroyed," which in the context is probably understood as emotional suffering, not physical.

TEV tries to show that the sufferings and hardships are not always present everywhere. It does this by using the modifiers "often...sometimes...many...at times." Other translations may find this helpful or even necessary.

4.10 RSV	TEV
always carrying in the body the death of Jesus, so that the life of Jesus may also be manifested in our bodies.	At all times we carry in our mortal bodies the death of Jesus, so that his life also may be seen in our bodies.

TEV begins a new sentence, instead of continuing the same sentence of verses 8-9, as RSV does.

always carrying in the body the death of Jesus: the meaning of this rather strange statement is made clear in the next verse. The apostles are always in danger of being killed because of their work of proclaiming the gospel. Here the death of Jesus means "the putting to death of Jesus," "the killing of Jesus." The translation can be "At all times we are in danger of dying as Jesus did" or "...of being put to death, as Jesus was."

so that the life of Jesus: there is here the implied condition of being saved from death. By surviving persecution the apostles are themselves evidence that Jesus is alive.

The verse may be translated as follows: "At all times we run the risk of being put to death, as Jesus was. And the fact that we are still alive serves to show that Jesus, too, lives."

[45]

4.11 RSV	TEV
For while we live we are always being given up to death for Jesus' sake, so that the life of Jesus may be manifested in our mortal flesh.	Throughout our lives we are always in danger of death for Jesus' sake, in order that his life may be seen in this mortal body of ours.

In essence this verse repeats, in clearer terms, the idea of the preceding verse.

while we live: the first person plural pronouns in this section (verses 7-12) refer to Paul and his companions. The translation of this clause may be "as long as we live" (TEV "Throughout our lives"). Or else, "We live, but we are always in danger of death...."

Always being given up to death means "always running the risk of being put to death." This happens for Jesus' sake (see verse 5).

The second part of verse 11 is like the second part of verse 10, except that instead of our bodies in verse 10, verse 11 has our mortal flesh. The meaning is the same, and here in verse 11 something like "our mortal body" (see TEV) may be better.

4.12 RSV	TEV
So death is at work in us, but life in you.	This means that death is at work in us, but life is at work in you.

The persecutions and sufferings of the apostles result in salvation and life for the Corinthian Christians.

death is at work in us: or "we (apostles) are always in danger of dying (or, of being put to death)."

The connection between the two parts of the verse can be stated as cause and result: "and because of this you have (spiritual) life."

As commentators point out, Paul is not ironical or bitter when he writes this; he is speaking the truth. Paul sees the sufferings of the apostles as a means of blessing and life for the Corinthian Christians.

4.13 RSV	TEV
Since we have the same spirit of faith as he had who wrote, "I believed, and so I spoke," we too believe, and so we speak,	The scripture says, "I spoke because I believed." In the same spirit of faith we also speak because we believe.

Paul now speaks of the unshaken faith the apostles have, which enables them to do their work. He quotes Psalm 116.10 in the way it appears in the ancient Greek version of the Old Testament, the Septuagint.

It is better not to follow the order of the text here, as RSV does, since this makes for a long and complex sentence. "The scripture says" (TEV) may be expressed by "It is written in the Scriptures."

"I believed, and so I spoke": it may be necessary to have an object for the verb "to believe": "I believed in God" or "I believed

God's promise." If an object for the verb in I spoke is required, the translation can be "and so I spoke about God (or, God's promise)."

the same spirit of faith: "Because we believe in the same way" or "Because we have the same kind of faith in God."

we speak: that is, we proclaim the gospel.

The verse may be translated as follows: "It is written in the Scriptures, 'I believed in God, and so I spoke.' We have the same kind of faith; we also believe and so we speak (or, proclaim the gospel)."

4.14 RSV	TEV
knowing that he who raised the Lord Jesus will raise us also with Jesus and bring us with you into his presence.	We know that God, who raised the Lord Jesus to life, will also raise us up with Jesus and take us, together with you, into his presence.

knowing: it may be better to begin a new sentence, as TEV does: "For we know," "For we are sure that."

he who raised the Lord Jesus: it may not be necessary in some languages to say explicitly, as TEV does, "God, who raised the Lord Jesus to life." But in other languages it may be important to name God as the one who raised the Lord Jesus.

raised: "made (him) live again," "made (him) alive again."

will raise us also with Jesus: by his statement with Jesus, Paul does not mean that God will raise Jesus again when he raises his people. The sense is that God, because he raised Jesus, will raise the believers. So in many languages it will be necessary to say "God...will raise us to life, as he raised Jesus."

into his presence: that is, into the presence of Jesus. Paul explicitly includes the readers, bring us with you; implicitly, this includes all believers.

The verse may be translated as follows: "For we know that God raised the Lord Jesus to life. We also know that he will raise us to life, as he raised Jesus. And then he will take us, together with you, into the presence of Jesus."

4.15 RSV	TEV
For it is all for your sake, so that as grace extends to more and more people it may increase thanksgiving, to the glory of God.	All this is for your sake; and as God's grace reaches more and more people, they will offer to the glory of God more prayers of thanksgiving.

it is all for your sake: "it is all for your good"; this is how Paul explains "together with you" in the preceding verse. All the troubles and difficulties that the apostles suffer, as described in verses 7-12, are for the sake of their fellow believers—in this case, the Corinthian Christians.

grace extends to more and more people: "as God's grace reaches more and more people" (TEV). Here this is specifically God's saving grace, that is, God's love acting to save people: "as more and more people experience God's love and are saved." For grace see 1.12.

it may increase thanksgiving: this is an impersonal way of saying "people will offer more prayers of thanksgiving." As the number of saved people grows, so will the number of thankful prayers increase.

to the glory of God: see 1.20.

The verse may be translated as follows: "It is for your sake that all of this happens. And as more people are saved by God's grace (or, as God, in his love, saves more people), more prayers of thanksgiving will be offered, to the glory of God."

SECTION HEADING

Living by Faith: "The Christian Lives by Faith," "We Are Always Full of Courage."

In this section Paul emphasizes the nature of the Christian life as faith that God keeps his promises. So the believer keeps looking at God and at eternal realities, and not to the human actions and temporary events of this world.

The confidence that believers have applies not only to what happens in this life, but especially to what happens after death. Whatever may happen in this life, the believer knows that in the life to come God will provide an eternal home.

4.16	RSV	TEV

So we do not lose heart. Though our outer nature is wasting away, our inner nature is being renewed every day.

For this reason we never become discouraged. Even though our physical being is gradually decaying, yet our spiritual being is renewed day after day.

So we do not lose heart: as at 4.1. In using the first person plural Paul has been speaking about himself and his companions as a group. In this section, however, what Paul is saying applies to all believers; consequently the inclusive first person plural forms should be used with all verbs in this section, 4.16—5.10.

our outer nature...our inner nature: here Paul distinguishes between the physical part of our being (literally "our outward self"), which is decaying, and the spiritual part ("our inner self"), which is being constantly renewed. The two may be referred to as "our physical being...our spiritual being" (TEV), or "our body...our spirit." Or else, "on the outside...on the inside," "outwardly...inwardly," "physically...spiritually."

is wasting away...is being renewed: "is decaying...is being made new," "is wearing out...is given fresh strength," "is getting weaker... is getting stronger."

every day: "continuously," "without stopping," "at all times."

Instead of making the sentence concessive, Though..., it may be easier to translate with two contrasting affirmations: "Our physical self, of course, is gradually decaying, but our spiritual self is constantly being renewed."

4.17

RSV	TEV
For this slight momentary afflic- tion is preparing for us an eternal weight of glory beyond all compar- ison,	And this small and temporary trouble we suffer will bring us a tremendous and eternal glory, much greater than the trouble.

this slight momentary affliction: for affliction see 1.4. Paul speaks of the difficulties and troubles of the apostles as being slight ("small," "insignificant," "little," "of little account") and momentary ("temporary," "do not last long," "disappear quickly").
is preparing for us: "produces for us," "accomplishes for us," "will bring us" (TEV). Paul is saying that the difficulties and troubles will bring us gain, not loss. And this gain is an eternal weight of glory beyond all comparison. The main problem here is to decide the exact meaning of glory in this context. It is interesting that the He- brew word for glory (kabod) means "heavy." So in using the phrase weight of glory Paul may have had this in mind, so that the phrase has the force of a superlative, "the greatest glory," "glory of the greatest kind." Here glory represents the presence of God and refers to the life of the redeemed in the immediate presence of God. The word should not be translated by "reward."
beyond all comparison: that is, there is no comparison between the glory in the future life and the troubles and difficulties of the pres- ent life. So TEV translates "much greater than the trouble."
The verse may be translated as follows:
The troubles we suffer do not last long, and they are small (or, insignificant) in comparison with what is to come. For they will bring us something far greater, which lasts for- ever, and that is eternal life with God.

4.18

RSV	TEV
because we look not to the things that are seen but to the things that are unseen; for the things that are seen are transient, but the things that are unseen are eternal.	For we fix our attention, not on things that are seen, but on things that are unseen. What can be seen lasts only for a time, but what cannot be seen lasts forever.

It is better, with TEV, to begin a new sentence at this verse.
we look: "we fix our attention" (TEV), "we keep our eyes fixed," "we never lose sight of," "we concentrate on."
things that are seen...things that are unseen: "what we can see... what we cannot see." The statement "look at invisible things" is not a logical one, but Paul's meaning is clear. It may be necessary to use some other verb: "keep our attention (or, minds) fixed on," "keep think- ing about." For the contrast between visible and invisible things, the translation could be "things of this life...things of the coming life," "physical realities...spiritual realities."

4.18

    <u>transient</u>...<u>eternal</u>: "last a while...last forever," "disappear...
endure forever," "temporary...eternal."

Chapter 5

5.1

RSV	TEV
For we know that if the earthly tent we live in is destroyed, we have a building from God, a house not made with hands, eternal in the heavens.	For we know that when this tent we live in—our body here on earth—is torn down, God will have a house in heaven for us to live in, a home he himself has made, which will last forever.

This verse continues without a break in thought from the preceding one. It continues to discuss the reason for believers keeping their thoughts fixed on spiritual realities. In verses 1-5 Paul speaks about the next life in terms of an eternal home, prepared by God, for every believer.

if: this may be taken as a way of putting the argument; so TEV translates "when." But if may have its full meaning, expressing a condition, since the belief was current among Christians at that time that the end of the world would take place within the lifetime of most people living then. Paul seems to have shared that belief (see 1 Thes 4.15-17).

the earthly tent we live in: Paul uses the phrase earthly tent to speak of the physical body, which will in time be destroyed. TEV has expressed the meaning of the phrase by "this tent we live in—our body here on earth."

is destroyed: the Greek verb is appropriate for a tent, which is "taken down," "folded," or "struck." The verb also means "destroy," and that is the meaning given by RSV and most other translations.

Such a figure of speech is not uncommon, but some languages may not have this kind of figure for the physical body. And so it may be necessary to say, simply, "For we know that when (or, after) we die."

In describing the believer's life after death, Paul uses words which emphasize the differences between the "home" there and the "home" here. There it will be a building from God, a house not made with hands. The word translated building means "a place to live in"; from God means "provided by God" or "made by God"; and not made with hands means it is not of human origin, but is of divine, heavenly origin. So TEV translates "God will have a house...for us to live in, a home he himself has made."

eternal: TEV "which will last forever."

If the metaphor "a house in heaven" (TEV) is difficult for readers, it may be necessary to speak of a spiritual body; Paul is talking about the differences between the physical body, of this life, and the spiritual body, of the life to come.

[51]

	RSV	TEV
5.2-3	Here indeed we groan, and long to put on our heavenly dwelling, 3 so that by putting it on we may not be found naked.	And now we sigh, so great is our desire that our home which comes from heaven should be put on over us; 3 by being clothed with it we shall not be without a body.

Here: or "In this situation," "While we live in this earthly house," "In this present body."

we groan: this is an expression of frustration, of sadness, of unfulfilled desire, explained by the next verb, and (we) long: "we wait with longing," "we earnestly desire," "we sigh with longing." TEV has "so great is our desire...."

to put on our heavenly dwelling: RSV translates the Greek verb as middle voice, to put on. In verse 4, however, it translates the same form as a passive, be further clothed. It seems better to take the verb here in verse 2 as a passive also, and so to translate "be put on over us" (TEV). It should be noticed that Paul is using figures that really do not go together: one does not "put on" a house like clothing. Paul mixes the two figures, referring to the spiritual body both as a home and as clothing.

For our heavenly dwelling TEV has "our home which comes from heaven"; or else, "our home in heaven."

by putting it on: or "by being clothed with it" (TEV), in the passive sense, not the active. In these passives God is the actor; it is God who will put the heavenly home on the believer.

not be found naked: here TEV gives the sense of the figure by "we shall not be without a body." The idea may seem strange and may be difficult to translate and express naturally. Paul thinks of the condition after death in which the person is a spirit without a body, either physical or spiritual. What Paul hopes for is that Christ will return before he dies, so that he will put on his spiritual body over his physical body, and not undergo the experience of being a disembodied spirit in Sheol, the world of the dead.

Verses 2 and 3 may be translated as follows:

While we live in this body (or, in this house on earth) we are unhappy and sigh, because we want the other body, the one from heaven, to be put on over us. 3 We want to be in our new body (or, our new home), and then we will never be without a body.

	RSV	TEV
5.4	For while we are still in this tent, we sigh with anxiety; not that we would be unclothed, but that we would be further clothed, so that what is mortal may be swallowed up by life.	While we live in this earthly tent, we groan with a feeling of oppression; it is not that we want to get rid of our earthly body, but that we want to have the heavenly one put on over us, so that what is mortal will be transformed by life.

In this verse Paul expresses more fully what he has been saying, explaining precisely why he wants to be clothed with the home from heaven.

in this tent: as in verse 1.

we sigh with anxiety: "we groan with oppression" or "we feel oppressed and groan."

not...unclothed, but...further clothed: Paul uses the figure of clothing; the physical body will be taken off (at death) and the spiritual body will then be put on. But what Paul prefers is that the new spiritual body be put on over him while he is still in his physical body, that is, that Christ will return and so this transformation will take place before Paul dies.

swallowed up: the same Greek verb which is translated overwhelmed in 2.7. Here the figure is that of the one set of clothing (the physical body) being absorbed by the new clothing (the spiritual body). TEV has "transformed." Instead of the passive form be swallowed up, it may be better to use an active form: "...so that eternal life will absorb (or, transform) our mortal bodies."

5.5 RSV	TEV
He who has prepared us for this very thing is God, who has given us the Spirit as a guarantee.	God is the one who has prepared us for this change, and he gave us his Spirit as the guarantee of all that he has in store for us.

prepared us for this very thing: that is, for this change of "clothing" or "housing," from physical and mortal to spiritual and eternal.

the Spirit as a guarantee: as in 1.22. Here the Spirit is the guarantee that this change from the mortal body to an immortal body will take place.

5.6 RSV	TEV
So we are always of good courage; we know that while we are at home in the body we are away from the Lord,	So we are always full of courage. We know that as long as we are at home in the body we are away from the Lord's home.

The assurance given by God's Spirit that the transformation will indeed take place fills the believer with courage: So we are always of good courage, or "We are always confident," "We do not lose hope," "We never become discouraged" (see 4.1,16).

at home in the body: or "live this physical life," "have this (physical) body as our home."

we are away from the Lord: life with the Lord Jesus Christ will be experienced fully only after death. In verses 6,8,9 Paul uses a pair of contrasting verbs three times: "be at home" and "be away from home." In this life a believer is home in the body; in the next life the believer is home with the Lord Jesus Christ.

5.7 RSV	TEV
for we walk by faith, not by sight.	For our life is a matter of faith, not of sight.

   we walk by faith, not by sight: here the verb walk means "to live" or "to act," as it often does in the Bible. The phrases by faith and by sight may be quite general, as RSV and TEV have translated them (see a similar statement in 4.18). But both may specifically relate to the Lord Jesus: "We live in this life by trusting (or, believing) in him, not by seeing him." Most translations are like RSV and TEV; not by sight means not being able to see with one's eyes the spiritual realities and forces which govern the Christian life.

5.8 RSV	TEV
We are of good courage, and we would rather be away from the body and at home with the Lord.	We are full of courage and would much prefer to leave our home in the body and be at home with the Lord.

   Paul repeats "We are full of courage" (TEV).
   would rather be: "would much prefer to" (TEV).
   be away from the body: that is, leave this physical life by being taken by the Lord Jesus at his return. Paul is not talking about death as a natural and inevitable end of life; he is talking specifically about the hope for the Lord's return, at which time the believer will be taken to the new life in heaven with him.
   at home with the Lord: "go live with the Lord Jesus."

5.9 RSV	TEV
So whether we are at home or away, we make it our aim to please him.	More than anything else, however, we want to please him, whether in our home here or there.

   at home or away: that is, in this life or in the next life. Wherever we are, here or there," "whether in this life or in the next life."
   we make it our aim to please him: "our greatest wish is to please him."
   The verse may be translated as follows: "So we want to do what pleases the Lord, wherever we are, whether we are still in our body (here in this life) or out of it (in the life to come, with him)."

5.10 RSV	TEV
For we must all appear before the judgment seat of Christ, so that each one may receive good or evil, according to what he has done in the body.	For all of us must appear before Christ, to be judged by him. Each one will receive what he deserves, according to everything he has done, good or bad, in his bodily life.

we must all: it may be that by saying "all of us" (TEV) Paul here consciously shifts from talking about himself and his companions, and for the first time speaks of all believers. But, as said above (see 4.16), it seems likely that Paul speaks in this section (4.16—5.10) of all believers and not just of the apostles.

appear: some take the Greek verb to have the meaning here of "reveal"; "everyone will be revealed," that is, the character, conduct, and actions will all be made known. So "we must all have our lives laid open," "all the truth about us will be brought out." But the verb is also used in the weakened sense of "to be present" somewhere, and this seems to be the meaning here.

the judgment seat of Christ: on the Day of Judgment everyone will be judged by Christ. Elsewhere Paul speaks of the judgment seat of God (Rom 14.10). TEV, instead of representing the object, the judgment seat, here expresses its function. "...appear before Christ, to be judged by him." Or else, "appear before Christ, who will judge all people" or "appear before Christ, the Judge of all."

receive good or evil: this would mean "be punished or be rewarded." But it seems more likely that the Greek phrase "either good or evil" goes not with the verb receive, as RSV has it, but with the verb he has done, as TEV has it. So TEV has "Each one will receive what he deserves"; or "...what is due to him." The Greek verb means "receive recompense (or, pay)."

what he has done in the body: "what he has done in this life," "what he has done while he lived here on earth."

The verse may be translated as follows:
For all of us will have to appear (or, be present) before Christ, our Judge. He will judge us and give everyone the reward or punishment he deserves. Christ will do this according to the good things or the bad things that each one of us has done in this life on earth.

SECTION HEADING

Friendship with God through Christ: "The Message of Peace," "The Task of Reconciliation."

It is difficult to find an appropriate heading for this long section, since Paul does not consistently develop one idea or follow a single theme. In 5.11-13 he again tries to convince the readers that he and his co-workers have always acted properly; in the rest of the chapter (5.14-21) he develops the idea of reconciliation as the message and task of the apostles. And in 6.1-10 he speaks eloquently of the sufferings and difficulties the apostles face in carrying out their task. And finally, in 6.11-13, he makes a pathetic appeal to his readers to open their hearts wide to him.

Some commentaries and translations end the section at 6.10, not 6.13; others divide this material into two or three sections: 5.11-21 and 6.1-10; or else, 5.11-17 ("New Persons in Union with Christ"), 5.18-21 ("Messengers of Peace"), and 6.1-13 ("The Task of an Apostle"). Either one of these two divisions of the material would be better than the one long section in TEV.

5.11 RSV	TEV
Therefore, knowing the fear of the Lord, we persuade men; but what we are is known to God, and I hope it is known also to your conscience.	We know what it means to fear the Lord, and so we try to persuade others. God knows us completely, and I hope that in your hearts you know me as well.

knowing the fear of the Lord: this means "We know what it means to fear the Lord" (TEV). Here, as elsewhere in the Bible, "the fear of the Lord" is an attitude of respect, reverence, and awe toward God, and not just of fright. The statement seems prompted by what Paul has just said about the Judgment. Here the Lord is the Lord Jesus Christ. Paul himself must be judged by Christ, and this knowledge fills him with reverence and awe.

we persuade men: "we try to convince people," either to accept the gospel, or else to believe in Paul's own sincerity and integrity. The verb "to persuade" should not be translated in such a way that makes Paul claim that his efforts are successful; in the nature of the case, he could only try to persuade people.

what we are is known to God: it is better to use the active form, with God as subject: "God knows us very well," "God knows everything about us."

it is known also: that is, what we are. Again, it seems better to use the direct form: "and I hope that...you know me as well" (TEV). Here Paul uses the first person singular I hope, which is why TEV has "know me"; others have "know us."

your conscience: Paul seems to use the word in order to appeal to the Corinthians' deepest feelings (see comments on 1.12; 4.2). Whether they may want to admit it or not, they should know, deep in their hearts, that Paul and his companions have always acted with integrity and sincerity. It may not be possible in some languages to say "you know this in your conscience" or "...in your hearts" (TEV), and so it may be necessary to say, simply, "and I hope that you also really (or, truly) know me (or, us)" or "...that you know me (or, us) as well as God does."

This verse may be translated as follows:

The knowledge (or, awareness) of the fact that we shall all be judged by Christ fills us with awe (or, fear). For this reason we try to convince people that we are sincere and true. God knows everything about me, and I hope that you also really know me that well.

5.12 RSV	TEV
We are not commending ourselves to you again but giving you cause to be proud of us, so that you may be able to answer those who pride themselves on a man's position and not on his heart.	We are not trying again to recommend ourselves to you; rather, we are trying to give you a good reason to be proud of us, so that you will be able to answer those who boast about a man's appearance and not about his character.

commending ourselves: see 3.1.

We are...giving you cause to be proud of us: "We are...explaining our actions (or, our motives) so that you can always be proud of us." For the idea of to be proud see 1.14. The passage 1.13-14 says much the same that is said here in 5.11-12.

to answer: here Paul is appealing to those in the Corinthian church who have defended him from accusations brought by others. Paul's enemies and critics boasted of outward appearances rather than of inner worth: "who can only boast about what they appear to be and not about what they are" or "whose pride is all in outward show and not in inner worth."
This verse may be translated as follows:
Don't accuse us of trying to recommend ourselves to you again. No, what we are trying to do is to give you a good reason for being proud of us. And then you will know how to answer those people who boast about a person's outward appearance, not about his character.

5.13   RSV   TEV
For if we are beside ourselves, it   Are we really insane? It is for
is for God; if we are in our right   God's sake. Or are we sane? Then
mind, it is for you.   it is for your sake.

if we are beside ourselves: "if we are crazy." Here it appears that Paul is quoting what others have said about him. "Am I really mad, as people say?" And then he gives the answer, "If I am, it is for God's sake." Paul is not admitting that he is insane; he only takes up the accusation of his critics in order to refute it. What they may consider madness on his part, Paul sees as his dedication to God.

if we are in our right mind: here it seems better to translate as an affirmation and not as a possibility. To translate as a possibility might mislead the reader into thinking that Paul was not sure he was sane. "But in fact we are sane, and it is for your benefit (or, for your sake)."

5.14   RSV   TEV
For the love of Christ controls us,   We are ruled by the love of Christ,
because we are convinced that one   now that we recognize that one man
has died for all; therefore all   died for everyone, which means
have died.   that they all share in his death.

the love of Christ controls us: the genitive phrase the love of Christ means "Christ's love for us" and not "our love for Christ." This is made clear by the immediate reference to Christ's death for all people. What Paul and his colleagues do is in response to Christ's love; they are kept from selfish and vain conduct by Christ's love for them. Some translations give the meaning "compel" or "urge" to the verb; but "rule" or "control" seems better.

because we are convinced: "because we have reached the conclusion." What Paul is convinced of is not that Christ died for all, but rather he is convinced of the conclusion he draws, namely, that Christ's death for all means that all died. It does not seem that because is the best translation of the relation between what follows and what precedes (see below for the suggested translation of the verse).

In an indirect way Paul speaks of Christ's death as one has died for all. It may be necessary to say: "the one person, Jesus Christ, died for all people."

It may be difficult if not impossible to say precisely what Paul means by therefore all have died. He is saying that the death of Christ, as a representative of all people, involved them all; somehow, as TEV says, "they all share in his death." This is based on the Hebrew concept that one person, a leader or a ruler, is so intimately identified with his people that what happens to him also happens to them. Obviously Christ's death was a physical death; the death of all is not the death of the body but the death of the old self (see especially Gal 2.19b-20). It may be more difficult to follow the form of the TEV rendering. The best way to handle the statement is perhaps to follow the literal form, "and so all people (also) died." But in some way, if possible, a distinction must be made between Christ's physical death and people's spiritual death.

The verse may be translated as follows: "We act as we do because we are ruled by Christ's love for us. He died for all, and we are convinced that the (physical) death of this one man for all people means that they have all died (spiritually)."

5.15	RSV	TEV
	And he died for all, that those who live might live no longer for themselves but for him who for their sake died and was raised.	He died for all, so that those who live should no longer live for themselves, but only for him who died and was raised to life for their sake.

Paul repeats he died for all. And the purpose of Christ's death is explained in clearer terms: "so that those who live should no longer live for themselves" (TEV); "...should not continue to live for their own benefit." This is what the death of all means in verse 14: death to the old way of living, and life of a new kind.

but for him who: again it may be better to specify: "but for Chirst, who...."

was raised: "was raised from death," "was raised to life" (TEV), "was made to live again." It may be necessary to specify God as the actor: "was raised to life by God."

The verse may be translated as follows:
Christ died for all people so that those who live the new life (or, live as his followers) should not go on living for their own good, but should live for Christ. For it was for their sake that Christ died and was raised to life by God.

5.16 RSV	TEV
From now on, therefore, we regard no one from a human point of view; even though we once re-garded Christ from a human point of view, we regard him thus no longer.	No longer, then, do we judge anyone by human standards. Even if at one time we judged Christ according to human standards, we no longer do so.

From now on: this seems to mean "From this moment right now." The meaning, however, is "From the time we came to know the true meaning of Christ's death." So the phrase refers to the time of becoming a Christian. The translation could be "Since we became believers (or, followers of Jesus Christ)."

we regard...from a human point of view: this translates the Greek "we know according to the flesh." "We do not form our opinion about any-one according to worldly standards"; or "Our opinion of people is not based on human ways of thinking."

even though: Paul admits that at one time he had "known Christ ac-cording to the flesh," that is, his opinion of Christ was based on a purely human way of reasoning. This seems to be a reference to his at-titude and actions when he, as an influential Jewish leader, did his best to destroy the Christian movement.

we regard him thus no longer: that is, ever since conversion. The verse may be translated as follows: "Since becoming believers, we do not evaluate (or, form an opinion of) anyone by worldly standards (or, a human way of thinking). It is true that at one time we judged Christ that way, but we don't do it any longer."

5.17 RSV	TEV
Therefore, if any one is in Christ, he is a new creation;⁹ the old has passed away, behold, the new has come.	When anyone is joined to Christ, he is a new being; the old is gone, the new has come.

⁹Or creature

if: the conditional form of the sentence is rhetorical, that is, it is a way of making an affirmation. TEV "When"; otherwise, "Every time that...."

in Christ: see 2.14. TEV "is joined to Christ"; or "belongs to Christ," "becomes a Christian."

he is a new creation: or, as the RSV footnote has it, "he is a new creature." The Greek noun is active in sense, "the act of creating," but it is also used in the passive sense of "created thing," "creature." Most translations, like the RSV footnote and TEV, have "a new creature." Others, like the RSV text, have he is a new creation, which means, "he has been created again (or, anew)," which does not differ significantly from "a new creature." Others translate "there is a new (act of) crea-tion," or "there is a new world." Everything considered, "a new person (or, being)" seems the best translation.

[59]

5.17

the old...the new: "old conditions (or, ways)...new conditions (or, ways)." Or, "the old (way of) life is gone; the new (way of) life has begun."

5.18	RSV	TEV
	All this is from God, who through Christ reconciled us to himself and gave us the ministry of reconciliation;	All this is done by God, who through Christ changed us from enemies into his friends and gave us the task of making others his friends also.

All this is from God: the change, the new creature, the disappearance of the old and the coming of the new—this is all done by God.

who through Christ reconciled us to himself: "who by means of Christ brought us back to himself." The verb "to reconcile" means to restore a personal relationship that has been broken (see 1 Cor 7.11); it does not indicate who or what caused the break in the relationship. In this case Paul is talking about how God has acted through Christ to bring humankind back into a relationship of friendship and love to him. Here us means all believers and, potentially, all people. Since in English "to reconcile" is a rather high-level word, TEV has "God...changed us from enemies into his friends" (see also Rom 5.10). Another way of saying it would be "made peace with us." There are idiomatic ways of speaking about reconciliation: "to snap fingers with someone again," "to sit with," or "to eat with."

through Christ: this kind of relationship may be expressed by "God caused it, Christ did it," or, "it was because of what Christ did that God caused us to become his friends again," or "...God changed us from enemies into his friends."

gave us the ministry of reconciliation: "gave us the responsibility of making other people his friends." Here us is the apostles.

The verse may be translated as follows:

God has done all this for us. And because of what Christ has done, God made us his friends again (or, God changed us from enemies into his friends). He has now given us the work (or, responsibility) of making all other people his friends also.

5.19	RSV	TEV
	that is, in Christ God was reconciling[h] the world to himself, not counting their trespasses against them, and entrusting to us the message of reconciliation.	Our message is that God was making all mankind his friends through Christ.[d] God did not keep an account of their sins, and he has given us the message which tells how he makes them his friends.
	[h]Or God was in Christ reconciling	[d]God was making all mankind his friends through Christ; or God was in Christ making all mankind his friends.

This verse repeats essentially what is said in verse 18. The introductory words, that is, simply indicate a more precise statement of what has already been said: "that is to say," "I mean by this," "this is what I mean."

in Christ God: this means "God, by means of Christ" (as in verse 18). As the RSV and TEV footnotes show, the meaning may be "God was in Christ," "God was present in Christ," which is usually taken to refer to Christ's divine nature. But the meaning in the RSV and TEV texts is more probable.

was reconciling: this does not mean that God is no longer doing this; the tense of the verb is required by the past tense in the preceding verse, God...reconciled us. But should it appear that God is no longer reconciling humankind to himself, it will be necessary to say "God is making (or, trying to make) all persons his friends."

the world: here "all humanity," "all persons," "everyone."

not counting their trespasses against them: this explains what is involved in reconciliation, that is, God does not keep an account of people's sins with a view to punishing them; God does not hold them guilty and deserving to be punished. The verb translated counting is a commercial term, meaning to keep an account (of credits and debits). If such a figure is not useful, the normal term for forgiveness may be used: "God forgives their sins."

trespasses is one of the words used for disobedience to God's law; "transgressions," "offenses," "sins" (TEV).

entrusting to us the message of reconciliation: essentially the same that is said at the end of verse 18.

The verse may be translated as follows:
What I mean is this: by means of Christ (or, because of what Christ has done) God is trying to make all people (in the world) his friends. He freely forgives and forgets their sins, and he has given us apostles the message to proclaim that he wants to make all people his friends.

5.20	RSV	TEV
	So we are ambassadors for Christ, God making his appeal through us. We beseech you on behalf of Christ, be reconciled to God.	Here we are, then, speaking for Christ, as though God himself were making his appeal through us. We plead on Christ's behalf: let God change you from enemies into his friends!

we are ambassadors for Christ: Paul is speaking about himself and his fellow apostles. An ambassador is an official who represents his or her government in another country. If the technical term for ambassador is available and understandable, it is a good figure to use; otherwise, "representatives of Christ," or "we represent Christ," or "we speak on behalf of Christ."

God making his appeal through us: "through us God himself is appealing to all people." As ambassadors for Christ the apostles are representing God, who is trying to reconcile all humankind to himself. So it is the same as if God were speaking directly through the apostles.

We beseech: "We beg," "We implore," "We earnestly ask."
be reconciled to God: "let God reconcile you to himself." The work
of reconciliation can be done only by God; it is God who reconciles
people to himself, and not they who reconcile him. The break in relationship is their fault, not his.

5.21	RSV	TEV
	For our sake he made him to be sin who knew no sin, so that in him we might become the righteous-ness of God.	Christ was without sin, but for our sake God made him share our sin in order that in union with him we might share the righteous-ness of God.

he made him to be sin who knew no sin: it is better to have two
separate statements: "Christ was without sin, but God made him to be
sin." The affirmation Christ knew no sin means that Christ did not sin
(see Heb 4.15; 1 Peter 2.22). "Christ never committed sin," "Christ
was not guilty of sin."
    The statement "(God) made him to be sin" is translated literally
by RSV and others. The difficulty is that linguistically speaking it
is impossible to say that God made a person, Jesus Christ, to become
what is linguistically an object "sin." The noun "sin," however, involves activity: it is an event noun; that is, "sin" always means
"someone sins." Linguistically the most logical solution would be to
say "God made Christ become a sinner." (See Gal 3.13, where Christ
"became a curse.") But this seems so unthinkable that no translation
consulted says this. Some take the word to mean "sin offering," but
this meaning is rejected by most. TEV has "God made him share our sin,"
but this is quite indefinite and may not be satisfactory in other languages. One translation has "God placed on him the burden of all our
guilt," which may be the best. Or else, "God treated him as though he
were a sinner."
    It is important that For our sake be placed so as to modify God's
action: "it was for our sake that God made him." Here our includes all
Christians.
    in him: see in Christ at 2.14.
    we might become the righteousness of God: the same linguistic
difficulties have to be resolved here. It might be that "we might become God's righteous people" is the meaning intended. TEV tries to
maintain the parallelism with the preceding part by translating "that
in union with him (Christ) we might share the righteousness of God."
Again, this is so indefinite as not to be very satisfactory as a model
for translation.
    Here the righteousness of God is in contrast with sin, and so may
have the moral and spiritual sense of "goodness," "the moral qualities
of God himself." Or else it may mean what it often means in Paul's
writings: "right relationship with God."
    Perhaps the following translation may serve as a model: "Christ
(himself) never committed any sin, but for our sake God treated him as
a sinner. As a result we, in union with Christ (or, by being followers
of Christ), are in the right relationship with God (or, are pleasing to
God)."

Chapter 6

6.1   RSV

Working together with him, then, we entreat you not to accept the grace of God in vain.

      TEV

In our work together with God, then, we beg you who have received God's grace not to let it be wasted.

Working together with him: this translates a present active participle in Greek, "working together"; there is no verbal equivalent to with him (TEV "with God"). Some believe the Greek means "As we apostles work together" or "As we work together with you"; but the majority of translations are like RSV and TEV.

we entreat: "we beg" (TEV), "we ask earnestly."

not to accept the grace of God in vain: thus translated, it appears as if Paul is speaking of some present or future manifestation of God's grace, of God's blessings. It seems certain, however, that Paul is talking about the grace of God which they experienced at conversion, and he is pleading with them that they not let it go to waste. To state it in positive terms: he is urging them to make full use of God's grace in their lives. This is the love that God has shown the Corinthians in their Christian experience.

in vain: "for nothing," "to be wasted," "not make use of."

It may be easier and more forceful to translate with a positive exhortation: "We work together with God, and so we beg (or, urge) you to make full use of the grace (or, love) which God has shown for you."

6.2   RSV

For he says,
  "At the acceptable time I have
      listened to you,
  and helped you on the day of
      salvation."
Behold, now is the acceptable time;
behold, now is the day of salvation.

      TEV

Hear what God says:
  "When the time came for me to
      show you favor,
  I heard you;
  when the day arrived for me to
      save you,
    I helped you."
Listen! This is the hour to receive God's favor; today is the day to be saved!

In Greek, verse 2 is a parenthetical statement, interrupting the flow of the sentence which begins at verse 1 and continues at verse 3. It is better to do as RSV and TEV have done and make verse 1 a complete sentence, and begin verse 3 as a new sentence.

For he says: "For God says" or "God has said." The quotation is from Isaiah 49.8, words which God spoke to his servant Israel. Paul quotes this passage to reinforce his exhortation in verse 1 that the Corinthians make full use of God's grace.

the acceptable time: this phrase has been interpreted in various ways: (1) "the right time," "the opportune (or, proper) occasion"; (2) "at the time when you needed me," "at a time of your need"; (3) "at the time of my favor" is the sense adopted by most translations. TEV "When the time came for me to show you favor"; or else, "When it was time for me to be kind to you." The phrase is parallel with the day of salvation in the next line: "the day for you to be saved (or, for me to save you)."

I have listened to you: this is not just listening, but responding, answering favorably. The second person singular you is God's servant Israel, in the Old Testament passage. Here the second singular is not Paul, but is to be understood as referring to God's people. It may be necessary to use the second person plural to avoid the implication that it refers to Paul. The two verbs listened to you and helped you are also synonymous.

In Paul's comment on the passage, the phrases acceptable time and day of salvation should be translated in the same way that they are in the quotation.

The following may serve as a way to translate this verse:
For God has said:
  "I heard you when it was time for me to aid you,
   I helped you when the day came for me to save you."
Listen! Now is the time for God to help! This is the day for God to save!

6.3   RSV   TEV
We put no obstacle in any one's   We do not want anyone to find
way, so that no fault may be found   fault with our work, so we try not
with our ministry,   to put obstacles in anyone's way.

From here to the end of verse 10 is one sentence in Greek. The material is easily divided into complete sentences, however, and RSV should not be imitated.

no obstacle: "no difficulty," "nothing that will impede the progress." The word translated obstacle means barrier, impediment, offense, obstruction. A literal translation such as RSV makes it appear that Paul claims he never puts difficulties in people's way, that is, in the way of their Christian development. Rather, it seems better to say, with TEV, "we try not to put obstacles" or "we do our best to avoid putting obstacles," in order to make it clear that Paul is saying what he tries not to do.

so that no fault may be found: it is better to put this in active form, "so that no one will find fault," "no one will criticize," "no one will blame." It seems better, with TEV, to reverse the clauses: "We do not want our work as apostles to be criticized, so we try not to offend anyone."

6.4   RSV

but as servants of God we commend
ourselves in every way: through
great endurance, in afflictions,
hardships, calamities,

               TEV

Instead, in everything we do we
show that we are God's servants
by patiently enduring troubles,
hardships, and difficulties.

we commend ourselves: see 3.1.

through great endurance, in afflictions, hardships, calamities: it
seems better, with TEV, to take the Greek, "in much endurance," as a
statement of the way in which Paul and his companions face afflictions,
hardships, calamities; so TEV "by patiently enduring troubles, hardships,
and difficulties." This first group of three consists of quite general
terms. The noun endurance means "bear up under," "steadfastly endure,"
"not be crushed by" (see its use in 1.6).

6.5   RSV

beatings, imprisonments, tumults,
labors, watching, hunger;

               TEV

We have been beaten, jailed, and
mobbed; we have been overworked
and have gone without sleep or
food.

The same form continues to be used in Greek: "in beatings, in
imprisonments," and so forth. A translation may choose to continue
verse 5 without a break from verse 4, as RSV does; but it may be better
to begin a new sentence, as TEV does. The six difficulties listed here
divide easily into two groups of three.

beatings: either mob action or court punishment, or perhaps both.

imprisonments: "being put in jail." See also 11.23.

tumults: these are popular uprisings, disorders caused by the apostles' preaching the gospel. So here, "riots," "uprisings," "mob actions."

The next group of three, labors, watching, hunger, describes sufferings caused by the intensity of the work and not directly by hostile
enemies.

labors: "toil," "overwork," "hard work."

watching: "sleeplessness," that is, not being able to sleep regu-
larly.

hunger: either not having enough food to eat, or else not taking
the time to eat.

6.6   RSV

by purity, knowledge, forbearance,
kindness, the Holy Spirit, genuine
love,

               TEV

By our purity, knowledge, patience,
and kindness we have shown ourselves to be God's servants—by
the Holy Spirit, by our true love,

Here Paul begins a list of the virtues that he and his companions
have demonstrated in their work. So it seems best to make a complete
stop at the end of verse 5 and begin a new sentence here.

[65]

Purity refers to conduct, which is blameless, faultless, proper. It is not simply the absence of immoral conduct, but the presence of integrity and principles.

knowledge: this should be made more specific: "knowledge of the truth," "knowledge of the gospel."

forbearance: this is an attitude of tolerance, of not reacting in anger to other people's mistakes or opposition. It is closely allied with the following word kindness. The four terms may be translated as follows: "our pure conduct, our knowledge (or, grasp) of the truth, our friendliness (or, goodwill), our kindness."

the Holy Spirit: this seems odd, for this is not a human virtue but is God's power, God's Spirit strengthening and guiding the apostles. Some translate "a spirit of holiness," a human virtue, but the majority have the Holy Spirit.

genuine love: "our real love for others."

It is to be noticed that in verse 6 TEV has "we have shown ourselves to be God's servants," which is taken up from verse 4 in order to avoid making the list too long. But in some translations this may not be necessary, and the list can go on without interruption, as in RSV.

6.7	RSV	TEV
	truthful speech, and the power of God; with the weapons of righteousness for the right hand and for the left;	by our message of truth, and by the power of God. We have righteousness as our weapon, both to attack and to defend ourselves.

truthful speech: or, as TEV has it, "our message of truth," that is, the gospel. This seems preferable: "the proclamation of the true message."

the power of God: in a very general sense, God's power that is always available to the apostles: "the power that comes from God" or "the power that God gives us."

weapons of righteousness for the right hand and for the left: the RSV translation could be understood to mean that the figure weapons of righteousness means weapons for fighting the battle for God's will, God's way; in this case, the translation could be "weapons for fighting for the gospel." Or else righteous conduct, a Christian way of life, are thought of as weapons, as in Ephesians 6.14-17 and 1 Thessalonians 5.8; in that case, "we have our good way of life (or, our righteous conduct) as our weapons." This seems to be the better way to interpret the phrase.

the right hand...the left: "to attack...to defend"; the weapon for attack, the spear, was held in the right hand; the shield, the defensive weapon, was held in the left hand.

6.8	RSV	TEV
	in honor and dishonor, in ill repute and good repute. We are treated as impostors, and yet are true;	We are honored and disgraced; we are insulted and praised. We are treated as liars, yet we speak the truth;

From here on Paul uses contrasting pairs. Again, with TEV, it is better to begin a new sentence here.

in honor and dishonor: "we are praised (by some) and denounced (by others)," "some people speak well of us, others speak ill of us."

in ill repute and good repute: "insulted by some, praised by others," or "having a good reputation with some people, but a bad reputation with others."

We are treated as impostors...are true: "People call us traitors (to the gospel), but we are faithful," or else "They say that we are liars, but we speak the truth."

6.9 RSV	TEV
as unknown, and yet well known; as dying, and behold we live; as punished, and yet not killed;	as unknown, yet we are known by all; as though we were dead, but, as you see, we live on. Although punished, we are not killed;

unknown...well known: here unknown probably has the meaning of "not worth knowing": "people say we can be ignored...," "people call us 'nobodies,' but everyone knows us (or, we are known everywhere)."

dying...we live: perhaps, as the American idiom has it, "we are as good as dead." The thought is not that people had said that Paul and his companions had died, but that they might as well be dead, for all the good they were doing. Or else, considering the severity of his sufferings, Paul is saying that he should be dead but is alive: "We are always in danger of dying, but as you see, we live on." What follows makes this interpretation the more probable one.

punished...not killed: it is difficult to decide whether Paul sees his punishment as divine discipline or as human chatisement. Probably human chastisement is correct: "We are severely punished, but we don't die."

6.10 RSV	TEV
as sorrowful, yet always rejoicing; as poor, yet making many rich; as having nothing, and yet possessing everything.	although saddened, we are always glad; we seem poor, but we make many people rich; we seem to have nothing, yet we really possess everything.

sorrowful...rejoicing: the formal contradiction is an emphatic way of saying that the pain and sorrows of their work cannot overcome their Christian joy: "in our sorrows we always have reason to be happy." It is not quite accurate to translate "we seem to be sad but are really happy."

poor...making many rich: here the idea is that the apostles are poor in a material sense, but they enrich others in a spiritual sense. This may need to be said explicitly, if making many rich will be understood by the readers to mean material wealth.

having nothing...possessing everything: again it is the same contrast: poor in a material sense, but rich in a spiritual sense (see 1 Cor 3.21-22).

6.11   RSV   TEV
  Our mouth is open to you,   Dear friends in Corinth! We
Corinthians; our heart is wide.   have spoken frankly to you; we
                                   have opened our hearts wide.

     In verses 11-13 Paul makes an eloquent appeal to his readers.
These verses fittingly conclude the section, which has dwelt on the
difficulties and troubles Paul and his companions have experienced in
their work.
     Our mouth is open: "we are speaking freely (or, frankly)."
     our heart is wide: "we have opened our hearts to you," that is,
we have not hidden our thoughts, emotions, wishes. "We have shown our
love for you."

6.12   RSV   TEV
You are not restricted by us, but   It is not we who have closed our
you are restricted in your own   hearts to you; it is you who have
affections.   closed your hearts to us.

     You are not restricted by us: "We have not closed our hearts to
you," "We are not restrained in our affection (or, love) for you."
     you are restricted in your own affections: "you have closed your
hearts to us"; "you have been restrained in your affection (or, love)
for us."

6.13   RSV   TEV
In return—I speak as to children   I speak now as though you were my
—widen your hearts also.   children: show us the same feel-
                                    ings that we have for you. Open
                                    your hearts wide!

     In return: that is, do the same for us that we have done for you.
     I speak as to children: "I speak as a father would to his own
children."
     widen your hearts also: "show (us) your love for us."
     It must be said that the RSV literal representation of verses
11-13 does not qualify as a clear and meaningful translation.

SECTION HEADING

     Warning against Pagan Influences: "Avoid Fellowship with Unbe-
lievers," "We Are the Temple of the Living God."

     This clearly-defined section abruptly changes the tone and content
of Paul's letter. The plea with which he ends the preceding section
(verse 13) is taken up again at 7.2. Many believe this warning to the
Corinthians against close fellowship with unbelievers (6.14—7.1) is
part of a previous letter, the one referred to in 1 Corinthians 5.9.
But in any case, in this section Paul exhorts his readers not to

maintain relations with unbelievers, but to continue faithful to Christ. In this way they will be the people of God, completely dedicated to his will and his purposes.

6.14 RSV

Do not be mismated with unbelievers. For what partnership
have righteousness and iniquity?
Or what fellowship has light with
darkness?

TEV

Do not try to work together
as equals with unbelievers, for
it cannot be done. How can right
and wrong be partners? How can
light and darkness live together?

<u>mismated</u>: this translates a verb which means "to yoke unequally" (see <u>KJV</u>), that is, to yoke together two animals that are not of the same kind and do not work well together, such as a donkey and a bull. The figure of being yoked may not be natural or intelligible, and so it may be better to use a verb like "unite" or "join together": "Don't be joined together with unbelievers," "Don't unite with pagans." But somehow the idea of work should be expressed, since animals are yoked together in order to work; and Paul is not talking simply of associating with unbelievers but of working with them. That is why TEV has "Do not try to work together as equals with unbelievers." TEV also has "for it cannot be done," in order to bring out the force of an unnatural, unworkable alliance. Other translations are: "Do not harness yourselves in an uneven team with unbelievers"; "Do not try to team up with unbelievers"; "Don't link up with unbelievers and try to work with them"; "Don't try to work with unbelievers; it would be like trying to harness two different animals together."

<u>unbelievers</u>: "non-Christians," "pagans," "people who do not believe in Christ."

In five successive rhetorical questions Paul shows that this kind of union is impossible.

<u>what partnership...?</u>: "there is no partnership," or "...cannot be partners," "cannot work together."

<u>righteousness and iniquity</u>: "right and wrong," "virtue and sin," "goodness and evil."

<u>what fellowship...?</u>: "there is no fellowship," "...cannot be friends," "cannot live together."

<u>light and darkness</u>: these two figures for good and evil, or life and death, are quite common, and most languages use them. However, if the figures are not natural or intelligible, it will be necessary to say "good and evil" or "virtue and sin."

6.15 RSV

What accord has Christ with Belial?[i]
Or what has a believer in common
with an unbeliever?

TEV

How can Christ and the Devil agree?
What does a believer have in common
with an unbeliever?

[i]Greek *Beliar*

6.15

What accord...?: "There cannot be any agreement..."; "...cannot agree," "cannot be in harmony with."

Belial: a name for the Devil (see 2.11). The RSV text uses the form corresponding to the Hebrew form of the word (which means "worthlessness"); as the RSV footnote shows, the Greek form is "Beliar."

what...in common with...?: "there is nothing they have in common." The context should make it clear that Paul is talking about matters of faith and morality. He is not saying that believers should isolate themselves totally from unbelievers and live in segregated communities where they would have no association with unbelievers.

a believer...an unbeliever: "a Christian...a non-Christian."

6.16

RSV	TEV
What agreement has the temple of God with idols? For we are the temple of the living God; as God said,	How can God's temple come to terms with pagan idols? For we are the temple of the living God! As God himself has said,

"I will live in them and move
        among them,
  and I will be their God,
  and they shall be my people.
	"I will make my home with my
	        people
	    and live among them;
	  I will be their God,
	    and they shall be my
	      people."

What agreement...?: "There is no agreement," "There can be no pact (or, contract)."

the temple of God: "the temple where (the true) God is worshiped."

idols: "false gods." Since the first element is "God's temple," it may be necessary to say here "an idol temple" or "a temple where idols are worshiped."

The five rhetorical questions of verses 14b-16a may be translated as follows:

Goodness and evil cannot be partners (or, work together)! Light and darkness cannot live together! There can be no agreement between Christ and the Devil! A believer has nothing in common with an unbeliever! The temple of the true God and idols (or, and a temple of idols) cannot become allies (or, form an alliance)!

we are the temple of the living God: Paul explains what he means by the word temple: it is the church, the fellowship of all believers. Here we includes all Christians. The "place" where God dwells is the Christian fellowship, the Christian community (see 1 Cor 3.16-17).

The quotation that follows is composed of a number of separate Old Testament passages. In verse 16 the quotation follows Leviticus 26.12 and Ezekiel 37.27.

I will live in them and move among them: the two verbs live and move mean the same thing, "to live with," "to have one's home among" (a people, or in a community); them refers to God's people. It is not necessary to have two verbs, but if natural and intelligible, two should be used, as TEV does: "I will make my home with my people and live among them"; or "I will live with my people."

I will be their God: "they will worship me as their God," "I will be the God they worship (or, serve)."

they shall be my people: "they will belong to me," "they will be the people I rule over (or, govern)."

6.17	RSV	TEV
	Therefore come out from them, and be separate from them, says the Lord, and touch nothing unclean; then I will welcome you,	And so the Lord says, "You must leave them and separate yourselves from them. Have nothing to do with what is unclean, and I will accept you.

The quotation in this verse expresses the thought of Isaiah 52.11 and Ezekiel 20.34. In the Isaiah passage God is speaking to his people who are in exile in Babylonia and commands them to leave that pagan country and return to their homeland. They were told to keep themselves ritually pure by having nothing to do with their pagan captors.

Therefore: RSV includes this as part of the whole quotation. TEV takes it as a link supplied by Paul, and not as part of the quotation. So TEV closes the quotation at the end of verse 16 and begins verse 17: "And so the Lord says." The words "the Lord says" come in the middle of the verse (see RSV). Since there is a change from the third person plural in verse 16 to the second person plural in verse 17, it will be better to begin verse 17: "And so the Lord says to his people."

come out from them: here it should be made clear in translation that them means the unbelievers, the pagan idol worshipers, something that neither RSV nor TEV does.

touch nothing unclean: in Ezekiel 20.34 the command is directed to the priests who would be carrying the holy vessels; they would have to keep themselves ritually clean so as to be able to carry the sacred items. Paul is using the words in a moral sense: "keep yourselves free from immorality," "keep yourselves morally pure."

I will welcome you: this is taken from Ezekiel 20.34 in the ancient Greek version of the Old Testament, the Septuagint. In the Old Testament passage the promise is that God will welcome the returning exiles back to their homeland. Here the promise is general and is explained by the quotation in the next verse. So RSV connects this last line of verse 17 with verse 18.

6.18	RSV	TEV
	and I will be a father to you, and you shall be my sons and daughters, says the Lord Almighty."	I will be your father, and you shall be my sons and daughters, says the Lord Almighty."

The quotation here is from 2 Samuel 7.14, where God promises through the prophet Nathan that he, God, will be with David's son and successor, Solomon.

    <u>I will be a father to you</u>: "I will be your father" or "I will be like <u>a father to you</u>." The promise here is like that of verse 16b. Here <u>you</u> is plural, God's people. The text in 2 Samuel has only "son"; <u>sons and daughters</u> here may have been suggested by the language of Isaiah 43.6.

    <u>Almighty</u> translates a word meaning "all powerful," "ruler of all," "sovereign."

Chapter 7

RSV	TEV
Since we have these promises, beloved, let us cleanse ourselves from every defilement of body and spirit, and make holiness perfect in the fear of God.	All these promises are made to us, my dear friends. So then, let us purify ourselves from everything that makes body or soul unclean, and let us be completely holy by living in awe of God.

we: all believers.

have these promises: "since God promised us these things," "since these promises were made to us."

beloved: "dear friends" (TEV), "dear fellow believers," "dear brothers and sisters."

every defilement of body and spirit: "everything that pollutes (or, dirties) body and spirit," "every physical and spiritual filth." It is to be noticed that TEV has "soul"; in a passage such as this, no distinction is intended between "spirit" and "soul."

make holiness perfect: here holiness is holy living, that is, the kind of living required of God's people: "lives that are holy," "lives that are governed by God's commands (or, God's will)"; or else, "lives completely dedicated to God."

in the fear of God: see 5.11.

The verse may be translated as follows:

My dear friends, God has made these promises to us. So then, let us make ourselves pure by getting rid of everything that makes our bodies and our souls impure. And in reverence for God, let us dedicate our lives completely to him (or, let us lead completely holy lives).

SECTION HEADING

Paul's Joy: "Sadness and Joy," "Paul's Happiness over the Change in the Corinthians."

Here Paul picks up where he left off at 6.13, and in verse 5 he goes back to an account of his activities, which he had broken off at 2.13. Paul was overjoyed when, in Macedonia, Titus met him with the news about the Corinthians' change of heart. They had repented of their former hostility toward Paul and were anxious to be reconciled to him. Paul's joy knew no bounds as he heard the good news.

7.2 RSV	TEV
Open your hearts to us; we have wronged no one, we have corrupted no one, we have taken advantage of no one.	Make room for us in your hearts. We have wronged no one; we have ruined no one, nor tried to take advantage of anyone.

Open your hearts to us: although the language is slightly different, the meaning is the same as what is said in 6.13: "Show us your love," "Receive us into your affection (or, hearts)." Here us refers to Paul and his companions as do the other first person plural pronouns in this section.

Paul bolsters his request with three statements about his and his companions' conduct in Corinth.

wronged: "done wrong to," "been unfair to," "acted unfairly toward."

corrupted: "ruined" (TEV), "spoiled," that is, undermined their Christian faith. The word could refer to morals, but it appears unthinkable that Paul should have to deny that he had corrupted someone's morals.

taken advantage of: "cheated," "exploited," "misled," This could refer to money matters; if it doesn't, it is unclear what specifically it refers to.

The verse may be translated as follows: "Show your love for us! (Or, Receive us into your hearts!) We have not done wrong to anyone; we have never ruined (or, hurt) the faith of anyone, or taken advantage of anyone."

7.3 RSV	TEV
I do not say this to condemn you, for I said before that you are in our hearts, to die together and to live together.	I do not say this to condemn you; for, as I have said before, you are so dear to us that we are always together, whether we live or die.

I do not say this: that is, when Paul defends himself, he is not trying to make the Corinthians feel ashamed about the way he has been treated by them.

to condemn you: "to criticize you," "to make you feel guilty."

I said before: see 6.11-12.

you are in our hearts: "we love you," "you are dear to us."

to die together and to live together: in the sense that neither death nor any circumstance in life will separate them. The translation can be "We love you so much that nothing can separate us, neither death nor anything in life."

7.4 RSV	TEV
I have great confidence in you; I have great pride in you; I am filled with comfort. With all our affliction, I am overjoyed.	I am so sure of you; I take such pride in you! In all our troubles I am still full of courage; I am running over with joy.

I have great confidence in you: "I feel very sure about you," "I don't have any doubts about you." Or else, "I can speak openly (or, frankly) to you," "I can be quite bold (or, candid) in talking to you." Regardless of the past behavior of some of them, Paul feels sure that they love and respect him, and are good and faithful Christians.

I have great pride in you: "I am very proud of you."

I am filled with comfort: here comfort (see 1.3-4) is "courage" or "optimism." Paul is not discouraged, nor is he pessimistic; he is hopeful.

affliction: see 1.4. TEV takes the phrase "In all our trouble" to modify both of the final statements of this verse; RSV takes it only with the last one, I am overjoyed.

The following may serve as a model for translating this verse:
I have the greatest confidence in you, and I am very proud of you. All the troubles we have gone through have not discouraged me; on the contrary, I am always filled with joy.

7.5
RSV

For even when we came into Macedonia, our bodies had no rest but we were afflicted at every turn—fighting without and fear within.

TEV

Even after we arrived in Macedonia, we did not have any rest. There were troubles everywhere, quarrels with others, fears in our hearts.

Macedonia: see 1.16; 2.13.

our bodies had no rest: Paul is talking about himself and his companions: "we were not able to rest." The same Greek noun for "relief" is used in 2.13, my mind could not rest. Here Paul is saying practically the same thing, that is, that he was worried, tense, anxious; he could get no rest or relief, so troubled was he over the situation in Corinth.

afflicted: see 1.4.

at every turn: "all the time," "without letup," "in every place."

fighting without: "quarrels all around us" or "quarrels with other people" (see TEV). The other people could have been unbelievers, or perhaps antagonistic fellow believers.

fear within: "private doubts," "inner anxiety."

7.6-7
RSV

But God, who comforts the down-cast, comforted us by the coming of Titus, 7 and not only by his coming but also by the comfort with which he was comforted in you, as he told us of your longing, your mourning, your zeal for me, so that I rejoiced still more.

TEV

But God, who encourages the down-hearted, encouraged us with the coming of Titus. 7 It was not only his coming that cheered us, but also his report of how you encouraged him. He told us how much you want to see me, how sorry you are, how ready you are to de-fend me; and so I am even happier now.

comforts: see 1.3-4.

the downcast: "those who are discouraged," "those who have lost hope."

As RSV shows, to follow the form of the Greek and have only one sentence for verses 6-7 makes for a long and complicated sentence. It is better to divide the material into two or three sentences.

and not only by his coming: or, as TEV does, end verse 6 with a complete stop and begin a new sentence here: "We are cheered up not only by his coming" or "We were cheered up not only because we met him (or, he met us)."

the comfort with which he was comforted in you: this formal correspondence of the Greek text makes little sense in English. A translation could be "but also by the fact that he had been cheered up (or, encouraged) by you" or "but also by his report of how you had cheered him up" (see TEV). Or else, "...the fact that he felt encouraged about you."

your longing: that is, either to be reconciled to Paul, or else to see him again.

your mourning: "your sadness over what had happened," "your regret that you had caused me trouble."

your zeal for me: either to defend the apostle against his critics, or else to carry out his wishes; thus, either "to defend me" (with TEV), or else "to support me." Perhaps "to defend me" fits the context better.

I rejoiced still more: "I was even happier (then)," or "I am all the happier now" (see TEV).

7.8	RSV	TEV
	For even if I made you sorry with my letter, I do not regret it (though I did regret it), for I see that that letter grieved you, though only for a while.	For even if that letter of mine made you sad, I am not sorry I wrote it. I could have been sorry when I saw that it made you sad for a while.

with my letter: the harsh letter, referred to in 2.3-4,9.

even if I made you sorry...I do not regret it: two different Greek verbs are used, as reflected in RSV (and see TEV "made you sad" and "I am not sorry"). The first verb is used in 2.2,4,5 (where RSV translates "to cause pain" and TEV "to make sad"); the second verb is used by Paul only in this passage. It means "to be sorry about (something)," "to regret," "to feel remorse." The conditional form is a way of making a statement, which could be translated, "I know that the letter I wrote you made you sad, but I'm not sorry I wrote it."

The rest of the verse can be understood in different ways, as RSV and TEV show. RSV I do not regret it (though I did regret it), for I see.... This is possible, but seems less probable than the meaning expressed by TEV. Instead of RSV though I did regret it, TEV has "I could have been sorry," which better reflects the meaning of the Greek conditional expression, "Even if I had been sorry." This may be taken to indicate a condition contrary to fact. Some translate "Even if I were inclined to be sorry..." or "I may have been sorry."

    I see that that letter grieved you, though only for a while: here RSV translates grieved for the same Greek verb that is translated in the first clause as made you sorry. TEV joins this statement immediately to what precedes: "I could have been sorry when I saw that it made you sad...."
    The verse may be translated as follows:

> The letter I wrote you made you sad, but I am not sorry I wrote it. I realize that the letter did make you sad, even though it was only for a short time, and so I might have felt sorry. 9 But, as it is, I am (really) glad....

Or the second sentence could be translated and linked with verse 9 as follows:

> I might have felt sorry at the time because I knew that the letter did sadden you, although it was only for a while; 9 now, however, I am glad.

7.9 RSV	TEV
As it is, I rejoice, not because you were grieved, but because you were grieved into repenting; for you felt a godly grief, so that you suffered no loss through us.	But now I am happy—not because I made you sad, but because your sadness made you change your ways. That sadness was used by God, and so we caused you no harm.

    Paul says he is glad he wrote the harsh letter, and explains why he is glad.
    As it is: "Now," "As things have turned out."
    I rejoice, not because you were grieved: "I am happy, but not because you were made sad (or, because I made you sad)."
    you were grieved into repenting: "your grief made you repent," "your sadness made you change your mind (or, change your ways)," or "your sadness made you turn to God." To repent is to change one's mind about something; in the Bible it is especially to change one's way of living, one's conduct. In translation, it is not enough to use a verb that indicates only sorrow, or regret, or remorse, or a feeling of guilt. In the Old Testament the verb usually translated "to repent" means "to turn (around)"; it means to make a change, that is, to turn away from sin and toward God.
    you felt a godly grief: it is difficult to translate in natural and meaningful language the Greek phrase "according to God" in verses 9,10,11. It is contrasted with "the world's grief" (verse 10). Some translate "you bore the grief as God intended," "You bore the grief in a way that pleased God." Or else, "this sadness was (part of) God's plan."
    you suffered no loss through us: it is better to use an active form, "we caused you no harm" (TEV) or "...no damage." The Corinthians were not spiritually hurt by the painful letter Paul wrote; instead they were helped.
    The verse may be translated as follows:

> So, as things stand, I am glad I wrote the letter. I am not glad that I made you sad, but that your sadness led you to change your ways (or, turn to God). Your sadness was according to God's will, and so we did not hurt you by what we did.

7.10 RSV	TEV
For godly grief produces a repentance that leads to salvation and brings no regret, but worldly grief produces death.	For the sadness that is used by God brings a change of heart that leads to salvation—and there is no regret in that! But sadness that is merely human causes death.

In the first part of this verse Paul uses words and phrases already used in verse 9: godly grief, repentance, and brings no regret. The noun salvation appears also in 1.6; 6.2.

worldly grief: this is contrasted with godly grief and may be translated "sadness that is merely human" (TEV), "sadness based on human feelings (or motives)."

death is spiritual death, as contrasted with salvation, which is spiritual life, life eternal.

The verse may be translated as follows:
For sadness that is according to God's will leads a person (or, us) to turn to God, and so brings salvation (or, spiritual life). And no one feels sorry about that! But sadness that is merely human leads to spiritual death.

7.11 RSV	TEV
For see what earnestness this godly grief has produced in you, what eagerness to clear yourselves, what indignation, what alarm, what longing, what zeal, what punishment! At every point you have proved yourselves guiltless in the matter.	See what God did with this sadness of yours: how earnest it has made you, how eager to prove your innocence! Such indignation, such alarm, such feelings, such devotion, such readiness to punish wrongdoing! You have shown yourselves to be without fault in the whole matter.

For see what...!: Paul exclaims over the change in the attitude of the Corinthians, a change brought about by their godly grief. It is better to make of this initial statement a complete sentence: "See what this sadness of yours has done for you" or "See how your sadness made you change."

earnestness: they had lost their previous indifference and were now earnestly trying to change things.

eagerness to clear yourselves: "desire to explain (or, defend) yourselves." Some take the Greek noun "defense" (or "explanation") to refer to the Corinthians' desire to defend Paul: "how eager to defend me." This is possible, but not very probable.

indignation: the Corinthians were now angry that they had had troubles with Paul.

alarm: this translates the word normally translated "fear" or "reverence." Here it appears to mean that they were fearful of the possible serious damage to the Christian fellowship. Perhaps it means they were afraid of God's punishment, or else of what Paul might do and say on his next visit to them.

longing: as in verse 7, to see Paul and be reconciled to him.

zeal: to do what was right; or else "dedication" to God and to the apostles.

punishment: the willingness to punish the wrongdoer (see 2.6-8). TEV "such readiness to punish wrongdoing."

At every point: that is, in resolving the whole difficulty; see at every turn in verse 5.

proved yourselves guiltless: "shown that you were innocent," "demonstrated your innocence," "cleared yourselves of any blame."

in the matter: Paul refers in a very general way to the troubles at Corinth; "in this affair (or, incident)."

The verse may be translated as follows:

Your sadness was (part of) God's will for you, and see what it did for you! It made you eager (or, willing) to act and prove that you had not done wrong. You became angry over what had happened, and afraid of what might happen still. It made you want to see me, it made you eager to defend me and to punish the offender. Throughout this whole affair you have shown that you were not responsible for what happened.

7.12 RSV	TEV
So although I wrote to you, it was not on account of the one who did the wrong, nor on account of the one who suffered the wrong, but in order that your zeal for us might be revealed to you in the sight of God.	So, even though I wrote that letter, it was not because of the one who did wrong or the one who was wronged. Instead, I wrote it to make plain to you, in God's sight, how deep your devotion to us really is.

although I wrote to you: the harsh letter (see verse 8).

the one who did the wrong: the offender in the church in Corinth (see 2.6-8).

the one who suffered the wrong: Paul himself.

your zeal for us: "your devotion to us (apostles)." The Greek word translated zeal is the same one translated earnestness in verse 11.

might be revealed to you: it is better to use an active verb, "I might make clear to you" or "that you might see clearly."

in the sight of God: see 2.17; 4.2.

The verse may be translated as follows:

When I wrote that letter, I wasn't concerned about the person who did wrong or about the person who was wronged. I wrote it in order to make clear to you that God knows that you are truly devoted to us.

7.13 RSV	TEV
Therefore we are comforted.	That is why we were encouraged.
And besides our own comfort we rejoiced still more at the joy of Titus, because his mind has been set at rest by you all.	Not only were we encouraged; how happy Titus made us with his happiness over the way in which all of you helped to cheer him up!

comforted: see the verb in 1.3-4, and also its use in 7.6-7.

RSV and TEV both connect this statement with what precedes. Some join it to what follows, but it seems better to do as RSV and TEV have done.

besides our own comfort: "in addition to our being encouraged," "besides being encouraged ourselves."

we rejoiced still more: "we were happier still," "we were made even happier."

his mind has been set at rest: "his worries were removed," "his doubts were banished, driven away," "his fears vanished." Or a positive statement may be preferred: "he was encouraged," "his hope was revived," "his spirits were lifted." It may be better to use the active form of the verb instead of the passive: "because you had all cheered him up," "you had all made his worries disappear."

The second part of the verse may be translated as follows: "We were indeed encouraged; but Titus' own happiness made us much happier still. He told us how you had all dispelled his worries."

7.14 RSV	TEV
For if I have expressed to him some pride in you, I was not put to shame; but just as everything we said to you was true, so our boasting before Titus has proved true.	I did boast of you to him, and you have not disappointed me. We have always spoken the truth to you, and in the same way the boast we made to Titus has proved true.

Paul explains how he had praised the Corinthians when he talked to Titus before sending him to Corinth, and how he, Paul, had not been disappointed. And just as he had always spoken the truth to the Corinthians, his boasting about them to Titus turned out to be true also.

if: the conditional form does not express doubt but is a way of making a statement: "I did indeed brag to Titus about you."

expressed...pride: see be proud in 1.14.

I was not put to shame: that is, the Corinthians did not disappoint him by the way they received Titus. "I was not disappointed"; or "you did not disappoint me" (see TEV); "you have not let me down."

everything we said to you was true: or "We have always spoken the truth to you" (TEV); or it might be effective to use the negative form here and in the next statement: "we have never lied to you, and in the same way our boast to Titus about you was not a lie."

boasting before Titus: this could be understood to mean that Titus was only present when the boast was made, not that the boast was made to Titus himself. It is better to do as TEV has done, "the boast we made to Titus."

7.15 RSV	TEV
And his heart goes out all the more to you, as he remembers the obedience of you all, and the fear and trembling with which you received him.	And so his love for you grows stronger, as he remembers how all of you were ready to obey his instructions, how you welcomed him with fear and trembling.

[80]

his heart goes out all the more to you: "his affection (or, love) for you is now even stronger (or, greater)." Titus had arrived in Corinth doubtful as to how the Corinthians would receive him. So he had been most pleasantly surprised by their warm reception, and his appreciation of them and love for them grew even stronger.

the obedience of you all: that is, Titus found that the Corinthians were ready to obey the instructions Paul had sent by Titus.

fear and trembling: this is a strong phrase. It occurs in only three other places in the New Testament: 1 Corinthians 2.3; Ephesians 6.5; Philippians 2.12. Perhaps it does not mean great fear, but is an exaggerated way of describing nervousness and anxiety about something. Here some translate "deep respect," "respect and reverence," "respect and submission." But the literal meaning may well be intended, for it is possible to assume that before Titus arrived in Corinth the Corinthians were beginning to feel guilty about the way they had treated Paul, and were genuinely afraid of the consequences (see the word translated alarm in verse 11). So it may be better to use a phrase or an expression that indicates fear.

Perhaps the following may serve as a model for translating the verse:

> Titus remembers how you received him with humility and respect (or, with fear and trembling), and how all of you were ready to obey his instructions. And so his love for you keeps growing stronger.

7.16 RSV	TEV
I rejoice, because I have perfect confidence in you.	How happy I am that I can depend on you completely!

I rejoice: "I am very happy now."

I have perfect confidence: the same kind of sentiment that is expressed in 7.4. "I am so happy now that I can depend on you completely."

Chapter 8

Christian Giving: "The Offering for the Needy Christians in Judea."

Paul now takes up a project in which he is deeply involved, the raising of money in churches that he visits. This offering is to be sent to Jerusalem to help the needy Christians there. For Paul this was no ordinary relief mission. By their generous offer the Gentile Christians in Macedonia and Achaia would show their feeling of oneness in the faith with the Jewish Christians in Judea. There is the one church of Jesus Christ, which includes people of all races and cultures. For Paul this was fundamental, and the generous offering would help strengthen this basic principle.

First Paul talks about the splendid example set by the churches in the province of Macedonia (verses 1-7), and then he encourages the church at Corinth to complete its plans for raising their offering (verses 8-15). Some translations have two sections, 8.1-7 and 8.8-15. If this is done, the heading of the first one could be "The Generosity of the Christians in Macedonia," and the heading for the second one could be "The Corinthians Are Urged to Be Generous Also."

8.1	RSV	TEV
	We want you to know, brethren, about the grace of God which has been shown in the churches of Macedonia,	Our brothers, we want you to know what God's grace has accomplished in the churches in Macedonia.

We want you to know: "We want to tell you," "We want to report to you."

brethren: "brothers and sisters," "dear fellow Christians."

the grace of God: see 1.12.

which has been shown in the churches of Macedonia: the Greek verb is "has been given," which may be understood in different ways. RSV has been shown interprets the text to mean that God's grace has been clearly present in the churches in Macedonia, shown by the way in which they had acted. TEV "what God's grace has accomplished in the churches in Macedonia" is somewhat similar but seems clearer. Others translate "how gracious (or, good) God has been to the churches in Macedonia," but this seems less probable.

[82]

8.2 RSV	TEV
for in a severe test of affliction, their abundance of joy and their extreme poverty have overflowed in a wealth of liberality on their part.	They have been severely tested by the troubles they went through; but their joy was so great that they were extremely generous in their giving, even though they are very poor.

It is better to begin a new sentence here, as in TEV. Paul shows what God's grace has accomplished in the churches in Macedonia. Although the Christians there were very poor, they were very generous in the offerings they raised for their needy fellow Christians in Judea.

in a severe test of affliction: that is, they have been severely tested by the troubles they have been through. For affliction see 1.4.

test: the idea is that sufferings and difficulties put people's faith and character to the test; that is, they serve to show whether or not the faith is real, the character is genuine. With such an outlook Christians can be sure that their troubles and difficulties are within God's overall plan for them.

In the Greek text the two elements their abundance of joy and their extreme poverty are treated as coordinate phrases, as RSV shows. It seems more likely, however, that they should be seen as contrasting elements: "although they are very poor, still they are very happy, and this caused them to give liberally." Or else, "Despite the difficult troubles they have been through, they are still very happy; and despite being very poor, they have been very generous in their giving." This seems to be the best way to understand this verse.

Paul's language is vivid: he speaks of "grave difficulty," "overflowing of joy," "very deep poverty," and "abundance of liberality."

The verse may be translated as follows: "Our fellow believers in Macedonia have been through severe troubles, but they are always very happy. They are also extremely poor, but they are very generous."

8.3-4 RSV	TEV
For they gave according to their means, as I can testify, and beyond their means, of their own free will, 4 begging us earnestly for the favor of taking part in the relief of the saints—	I can assure you that they gave as much as they could, and even more than they could. Of their own free will 4 they begged us and pleaded for the privilege of having a part in helping God's people in Judea.

The sentence in Greek begins at verse 3 and goes to the end of verse 6. RSV makes a full stop at the end of verse 5, and TEV has two sentences in verses 3-4. Translators will take care to keep the sentences relatively simple, and the relation between the various elements clear.

they gave according to their means...and beyond their means: "they gave as much as they could, and even more than they could" (TEV). There is a formal contradiction here, but this kind of exaggeration is quite natural in many languages. Should this appear absurd in some language, however, it is possible to say "they gave all that they could; it seemed they gave more than they possibly could."

as I can testify: "I can assure you," "I tell you."

of their own free will: "without being forced to do so." RSV takes this with what precedes; TEV follows the UBS Greek New Testament text and connects this phrase with what follows. Either one makes good sense. If RSV is followed, it would be better to place the phrase earlier in the sentence: "I can assure you that of their own free will they gave..." or "...that they willingly gave...." If TEV is followed, a new sentence should begin: "They spontaneously begged..." or "Without anyone telling them to do so, they begged...."

the favor: "the privilege" (TEV), "the opportunity."

the relief of the saints: "to help their fellow believers (or, their fellow Christians)," "to help God's people." TEV has "God's people in Judea," to make clear who are the saints (see 1.1) who are being helped (see 1.16).

	RSV	TEV
8.5	and this, not as we expected, but first they gave themselves to the Lord and to us by the will of God.	It was more than we could have hoped for! First they gave themselves to the Lord; and then, by God's will they gave themselves to us as well.

and this: this is not very clear in English. It means "and this offering of theirs," "this action of theirs." Or, linking up with what follows, "And they did this, not as we expected, but...."

we expected: it is better to say "we hoped," as in TEV. "They did more than we had hoped for. First...."

they gave themselves to the Lord and to us by the will of God: it is better to separate to the Lord from to us: "first they gave themselves to the Lord," that is, they submitted themselves to the will of the Lord Jesus Christ, or gave themselves completely to the Lord's service. If it is not possible to speak of giving oneself, it is possible to say "they promised (or, pledged themselves) to do the Lord's will" or "...to serve the Lord Jesus Christ in all ways." And then, as TEV does, the rest can be stated thus: "and then, by God's will, they gave themselves to us as well." After pledging themselves to the Lord's service, the Corinthians promised Paul and his companions that they would willingly do whatever they proposed. For "by God's will" one can say "in obedience to God's will" or "following God's command." Or, "and then they promised us that they would follow our instructions, as God wanted them to do."

	RSV	TEV
8.6	Accordingly we have urged Titus that as he had already made a beginning, he should also complete among you this gracious work.	So we urged Titus, who began this work, to continue it and help you complete this special service of love.

we have urged Titus: "we begged Titus."

as he had already made a beginning: Titus had started the campaign in the church in Corinth to raise an offering for the needy believers in Judea. So Paul urged him to go on and complete this gracious work, "this special service of love" (TEV), "this generous action," "this act of Christian love."

The verse may be translated as follows:

Titus had begun among you the work of raising a generous offering, and so we urged him to go on and finish the project.

8.7 RSV	TEV
Now as you excel in everything— in faith, in utterance, in knowledge, in all earnestness, and in your love for us—see that you excel in this gracious work also.	You are so rich in all you have: in faith, speech, and knowledge, in your eagerness to help and in your love for us.e And so we want you to be generous also in this service of love.
	eyour love for us; *some manuscripts have* our love for you.

Here Paul urges the Corinthians to be generous; and to enforce his request he praises them for their excellence in Christian virtues.

as you excel in everything...see that you excel in this gracious work also: as RSV has it, the conclusion to the statement comes quite a distance from the beginning. It may be better, with TEV, to list first the qualities which Paul praises, and then his request to them. "You are ahead of others in everything you have (or, You are outstanding in everything), and we want you to be first also in this service of love."

faith: the Corinthians' faith in Christ is stronger.

utterance...knowledge: see 1 Corinthians 1.5.

all earnestness: see 7.11. TEV has "your eagerness to help." Some translate "enthusiasm."

your love for us: as the TEV footnote shows, many Greek manuscripts and ancient versions have "our love for you." This is harder to understand, and on the assumption that the more difficult text is likely to be original, UBS Greek New Testament prefers this text. Some who follow this text translate "the love which we have stirred up in you." This is possible but does not seem likely. It seems that the meaning is "our love for you," that is, Paul and his companions love the Corinthians more than they love other believers. But the text followed by RSV and TEV seems preferable.

The verse may be translated as follows:

In everything you are ahead of other Christians: in your faith in Christ, in your proclamation of the gospel, in your knowledge of the truth, in your willingness to serve, and in your love for us. And so I want you to be ahead of others also in this act of Christian love.

	RSV	TEV
8.8	I say this not as a command, but to prove by the earnestness of others that your love also is genuine.	I am not laying down any rules. But by showing how eager others are to help, I am trying to find out how real your own love is.

I say this not as a command: "I am not trying to order (or, tell) you what to do," "This is not an order." Paul refrains from appearing like a dictator (see 1.24).

to prove...that your love also is genuine: here to prove does not mean "to show" or "to demonstrate" as an accomplished fact, because the offering had not been taken up yet. There is here the element of intent or purpose: "but in order to find out," or, seen from a different point of view, "but to give you a chance to show (or, prove)."

by the earnestness of others: that is, Paul points out how well the churches in Macedonia responded to the call, and this serves as a challenge for the church at Corinth to do the same.

The following may serve as a model for translating this verse:

I don't say this as an order. Rather, by showing how eagerly the churches in Macedonia gave, I am trying to find out how real your love is.

Or,

This is not an order. But by using the eagerness of the churches in Macedonia as an example, I am giving you the chance to show that your love is real.

	RSV	TEV
8.9	For you know the grace of our Lord Jesus Christ, that though he was rich, yet for your sake he became poor, so that by his poverty you might become rich.	You know the grace of our Lord Jesus Christ; rich as he was, he made himself poor for your sake, in order to make you rich by means of his poverty.

you know: not simply to know as a piece of information, but to know from personal experience.

the grace of our Lord Jesus Christ: "the great love of our Lord Jesus Christ." (See also 1.12.)

he was rich: this is meant in a spiritual sense and, as the contrast with the following he became poor makes clear, it is a reference to Christ's existence before coming to the world, his sharing the power and the glory of God. A similar thought is expressed in Philippians 2.6-8. Christ became poor by becoming mortal man, giving up the power and glory he enjoyed with the Father in the heavenly realm.

by his poverty: Christ's "poverty" was his lowly state as a human being and living a life of humble service which ended with death on the cross. This is how Christ's poverty enables people to become rich in a spiritual sense.

It is clear that you, your, and you in this verse refers to the Corinthian Christians; but it should not appear that they alone, or they in a special way, were enabled to become rich as a result of

Christ's "poverty." If this is the impression that readers will get from the text, it will be better to use the inclusive first person plural "we" and "our." What is true of the Corinthian Christians is true of all Christians.

The verse may be translated as follows:

You know how great is the love of our Lord Jesus Christ for us. In his divine existence he was (spiritually) rich, but for your sake (or, in order to save you) he came to the world and was poor. He did this so that you could become spiritually rich.

8.10 RSV	TEV
And in this matter I give my advice: it is best for you now to complete what a year ago you began not only to do but to desire,	My opinion is that it is better for you to finish now what you began last year. You were the first, not only to act, but also to be willing to act.

in this matter: that is, the matter of raising a generous offering for the needy fellow believers in Judea.

I give my advice: "this is my opinion," "I think this is what you should do." Paul does not want to appear to be dictating to them.

it is best for you now to complete: it seems better, with TEV, to make a complete sentence of what Paul is recommending to his readers: "...it is better for you to finish now what you began last year." The year before, the Christians in Corinth had begun raising the offering for the needy believers in Judea. Apparently the dispute with Paul stopped the project, and now that the controversy is over, Paul recommends that they finish raising the money.

a year ago: it is better, with TEV, to say "last year."

you began: it is to be noticed that RSV has no equivalent to TEV "You were the first...to act." The compound Greek verb means not only "to begin" but "to begin ahead" (of someone else). Paul is saying that they had been the first to begin raising the offering.

you began not only to do but to desire: "you began to make plans and to act." Or, "you started not only to act but to act with enthusiasm."

8.11 RSV	TEV
so that your readiness in desiring it may be matched by your completing it out of what you have.	On with it, then, and finish the job! Be as eager to finish it as you were to plan it, and do it with what you now have.

RSV's formal equivalence is difficult to understand. In this verse Paul says three things to his readers: (1) finish the project; (2) show the same eagerness to finish it that you did to start it; (3) give as much as you are able to give. TEV "On with it, then, and finish the job!"; or "Finish the project now," "You ought to finish raising the money."

8.11

TEV "Be as eager to finish it as you were to plan it": "Complete it as eagerly as you planned it," "You were willing to plan it; be just as willing to finish it."

TEV "do it with what you now have": "do it in accordance with your resources," "give according to your means," or, more generally, "give as much as you can."

8.12 RSV	TEV
For if the readiness is there, it is acceptable according to what a man has, not according to what he has not.	If you are eager to give, God will accept your gift on the basis of what you have to give, not on what you don't have.

Again RSV is not easy to understand.

if the readiness is there, it is acceptable: this says that a person's readiness to give is acceptable; what should be said is that the gift that a person makes is acceptable to God if there is a spirit of willingness, or eagerness, to give. So TEV "If you are eager to give, God will accept your gift." Or, "If someone really wants to give, God (gladly) accepts the gift."

Paul adds that what matters is not the amount given; God wants each to give in proportion to his possessions. Some should give more than others; but the larger gifts are not necessarily more acceptable to God than the smaller gifts.

The following may serve as a model for translating this verse:
If you are eager to give, God will be pleased with the gift; that is, if you give as much as you can. God does not expect you to give what you don't have.

8.13-14 RSV	TEV
I do not mean that others should be eased and you burdened, 14 but that as a matter of equality your abundance at the present time should supply their want, so that their abundance may supply your want, that there may be equality.	I am not trying to relieve others by putting a burden on you; but since you have plenty at this time, it is only fair that you should help those who are in need. Then, when you are in need and they have plenty, they will help you. In this way both are treated equally.

It is to be noticed that TEV has verses 13 and 14 together; this is because it has not strictly kept the contents of the text within the limits of each verse, according to the Greek text that it follows (UBS Greek New Testament). In this text the clause that TEV translates "In this way both are treated equally" comes at the end of verse 13 and is repeated (in a slightly different form) at the end of verse 14. However, in the Greek text translated by RSV, the clause that RSV translates but that as a matter of equality comes at the beginning of verse 14. It is only a difference as to where the verse number 14 is placed; there is no difference in the text itself.

It is possible to follow the verse division of the Greek text translated by TEV without having to rearrange the order of the clauses: "I am not trying to put a heavy burden on you and a light burden on others; rather, I want all to be treated equally." By telling the Corinthians that they should give to the Jewish believers in Judea as much as they could, Paul might appear to be requiring Gentile Christians to do what Jewish Christians were not being required to do. But, as Paul clearly explains in the next verse, the time would come when the Gentile Christians would be in need, and then the Jewish Christians would be called upon to help.

your abundance at the present time should supply their want: it is better to make a sentence out of this: "You have plenty (or, are well off) now, and they have little (or, are in need), so you should help them."

so that their abundance may supply your want: implied here is the probability that the time will come when the conditions will be reversed: "When the time comes that you have little (or, are in need) and they have much (or, are well off), then they will help you."

that there may be equality: here Paul repeats what he has said at the end of verse 13. "In this way all are treated equally"; or, in idiomatic language, "It is a matter of share and share alike."

8.15 RSV	TEV
As it is written, "He who gathered much had nothing over, and he who gathered little had no lack."	As the scripture says, "The one who gathered much did not have too much, and the one who gathered little did not have too little."

As it is written: "As the scripture says" (TEV).

The quotation from Exodus 16.18 does not apply very naturally to what Paul is saying. As the Israelites in the desert gathered manna, they were told exactly how much each one was to gather (Exo 16.16). Some, as a matter of fact, gathered more than they needed, while others gathered less; but when they came to measure what they had gathered, it turned out that each one had the exact amount that had been set. The equality that the apostle is recommending is one of mutual sharing of resources, which was not the situation of the Israelites in the desert. In a general way the Old Testament incident illustrates Paul's contention that Christians should share equally; there should not be poor Christians and rich Christians.

gathered much...gathered little: it may be necessary to fill in, "gathered much manna...gathered little manna"; if the word "manna" should prove a problem, it may be necessary to say "gathered much food...gathered little food."

had nothing over...had no lack: "did not have too much...did not have too little" (TEV).

[89]

8.16

SECTION HEADING

Titus and His Companions: "Paul's Companions Will Help the Corinthians to Gather the Offering."

In this section Paul makes the arrangements for taking up the offering in Corinth. His colleague Titus and two other trusted companions will help gather the offering and then will take it to Judea. The possibility that Paul himself will go to Corinth with them is taken up in the next chapter.

8.16 RSV	TEV
But thanks be to God who puts the same earnest care for you into the heart of Titus.	How we thank God for making Titus as eager as we are to help you!

thanks be to God: "let us thank God," "we thank God."
same earnest care for us: here earnest care translates the Greek word that in 7.11; 8.7,8 is translated earnestness, and in 7.12 zeal. And here same refers to the quality of eagerness, or concern, that Paul and his companions have. It is better to make this explicit, as TEV does: "as eager as we are to help you," or "as eager to help you as we are." Or, it may be better, as some translations do, to refer this to Paul: "...as I am."
puts...into the heart of Titus: in some languages it may be natural and appropriate to translate literally, as RSV has done; in other languages it may be better to state it as TEV has done. "We thank God that he has made Titus just as anxious to help you as I am (or, as we are)."

8.17 RSV	TEV
For he not only accepted our appeal, but being himself very earnest he is going to you of his own accord.	Not only did he welcome our request; he was so eager to help that of his own free will he decided to go to you.

not only...but: this kind of construction may be difficult to imitate, and it may be better to use two positive statements; "He accepted my request to go to you; as a matter of fact, he was so anxious to do so that he had already volunteered to go."
our appeal: here, as elsewhere in this letter, a translator may wish to use the plural form our, referring to Paul and his companions, or the singular my, referring to Paul alone.
very earnest: this is the comparative form of the adjective "earnest" or "eager," which is related to the noun translated earnest care in verse 16.
of his own accord: this translates the same Greek word translated of their own free will in 8.3.

8.18	RSV	TEV
	With him we are sending the brother who is famous among all the churches for his preaching of the gospel;	With him we are sending the brother who is highly respected in all the churches for his work in preaching the gospel.

Titus will have two companions when he goes to Corinth; one is the brother who is famous among all the churches. There are many guesses as to who this man was, but no certainty is possible. From the way Paul refers to him, the Corinthians knew who he was. It is generally assumed that the brother is used in the Christian sense, "the fellow believer," "the Christian brother," and not in the natural sense of brothers with the same parents.

famous: "well known," "highly praised."

his preaching of the gospel: the Greek text says only "in the gospel"; a verb such as "preach" or "spread" or "serve" will have to be used.

8.19	RSV	TEV
	and not only that, but he has been appointed by the churches to travel with us in this gracious work which we are carrying on, for the glory of the Lord and to show our good will.	And besides that, he has been chosen and appointed by the churches to travel with us as we carry out this service of love for the sake of the Lord's glory and in order to show that we want to help.

Paul adds that this unnamed companion has been officially authorized by the churches to work with Paul in raising and administering the offering.

not only that: "in addition," "besides that" (TEV), "also." Besides his fame, this Christian leader has been chosen by the churches for this work.

appointed: TEV has "chosen and appointed," which is defensible but not required; the verb means "to elect by the raising of hands." Here "elected," or "chosen," or "designated" would be suitable.

the churches: churches in the province of Macedonia.

to travel with us in this gracious work: this translates "our traveling companion in this grace." Here the Greek work for "grace" stands for the Christian work that Paul and his companions are doing. TEV has "this service of love"; or else, "this Christian ministry." Instead of the Greek preposition for "in" with "this grace," many Greek manuscripts and ancient versions have the preposition "with," which makes the text mean "to travel with us as we take this (Christian) gift," that is, the offering. The manuscript support for "with" seems a bit stronger than for "in"; and it seems better to translate "to take this gift (or, offering)."

which we are carrying on: this sense goes well with the preposition "in"; with the preposition "with," however, the sense is "which we are administering" or "handling," or "which we are in charge of."

for the glory of the Lord: "in order to bring honor to the Lord Jesus Christ."

to show our good will: here good will translates the word translated readiness in verses 11,12. The translation here could be "our readiness to help," "our desire to be of service," "how eager we are to help."

The verse may be translated as follows:

Not only is he well known, but he was also especially chosen by the churches to accompany us on our travels. He will help us manage this love offering we are raising, which will bring glory to the Lord Jesus Christ and will show that we are eager to help our needy fellow Christians.

8.20	RSV	TEV
We intend that no one should blame us about this liberal gift which we are administering.		We are being careful not to stir up any complaints about the way we handle this generous gift.

We intend: the Greek word is a strong one and has the idea of being cautious, of taking care.

blame us: "criticize us," "find fault with us," "accuse us of wrongdoing."

about this liberal gift which we are administering: Paul is saying that he is doing everything possible to avoid being criticized for the way he is handling the generous gift. It is not, as RSV makes it seem, a criticism about the gift itself. So TEV "...complaints about the way we handle this generous gift."

8.21	RSV	TEV
for we aim at what is honorable not only in the Lord's sight but also in the sight of men.		Our purpose is to do what is right, not only in the sight of the Lord, but also in the sight of man.

It is better, with TEV, to have a full stop at the end of verse 20 and begin a new sentence here. Paul's words have an obvious relation to the Greek version (the Septuagint) of Proverbs 3.4. Paul intends to do not only what the Lord (here a reference to God) considers right, but also what is good and right from the human point of view. Paul wants his good motives to be apparent not only to God but also to his fellow believers. It would be easy for someone to accuse Paul of raising the money for his own benefit (see 12.16-18).

8.22	RSV	TEV
And with them we are sending our brother whom we have often tested and found earnest in many matters, but who is now more earnest than ever because of his great confidence in you.		So we are sending our brother with them; we have tested him many times and found him always very eager to help. And now that he has so much confidence in you, he is all the more eager to help.

with them: with Titus and the unnamed famous brother of verse 18.

our brother: another Christian, also unnamed. Here the Greek has the possessive "our brother"; again, it is assumed that this means a fellow Christian, as in verse 18. TEV "our brother" is difficult to understand; "with them" refers to Titus and the unnamed brother of verse 18. It would be better to say "we are sending another Christian brother with them." The our here means "of us believers"; it is inclusive.

tested: that is, by assigning various tasks and responsibilities, and seeing how well he performed them. If the idea of testing is difficult to express, it is possible to represent the meaning in this fashion: "he has demonstrated to us often that he is always ready to help."

earnest...more earnest: as in verses 16,17.

in many matters: this is probably a way of saying "in everything." So TEV "always very eager to help."

great confidence: see 3.4. This unnamed Christian leader is sure that his fellow believers in Corinth will cooperate willingly in raising the offering.

8.23 RSV	TEV
As for Titus, he is my partner and fellow worker in your service; and as for our brethren, they are messengers*j* of the churches, the glory of Christ. *j* Greek *apostles*	As for Titus, he is my partner and works with me to help you; as for the other brothers who are going with him, they represent the churches and bring glory to Christ.

Paul finishes talking about the men who are going to Corinth, making a summary statement about them.

Titus...is my partner: "...my colleague," "...my companion."

and fellow worker: "who works with me." If necessary, one could say "and works with me in proclaiming the gospel."

in your service: "to serve you," "to help you." This Christian ministry is not restricted to spiritual matters.

our brethren: that is, the two unnamed Christian brothers (verses 18,22) who are going with Titus. So TEV "the other brothers who are going with him"; or "the two fellow Christians who are going with him."

messengers of the churches: as the RSV footnote shows, the Greek word is the one ordinarily translated "apostles." Here it means authorized delegates, official representatives.

the glory of Christ: as RSV shows, the Greek has no separate verb with this phrase. The idea is that they bring glory, or honor, to Christ by the work they are doing.

The verse may be translated as follows:

Titus, please remember, is my partner, and he and I work together for your good. The two fellow believers who are going with him are representatives of the churches, and their work brings honor to Christ.

8.24 RSV	TEV
So give proof, before the churches, of your love and of our boasting about you to these men.	Show your love to them, so that all the churches will be sure of it and know that we are right in boasting about you.

RSV is not very clear. Paul tells his readers: (1) show that your love for these men is real; (2) this will show that when we boasted about you we were speaking the truth. The Macedonian churches will hear about it and will be convinced that Paul had been speaking the truth about the Corinthian Christians.

give proof...of your love: by receiving Titus and his companions warmly and cooperating with them in raising the offering. Here your love could be the Corinthians' love for Paul or their love for Titus and his companions.

before the churches: in such a way that the churches in Macedonia would hear about it.

boasting: see 1.14, the discussion on proud.

about you to these men: this is possible, but it seems better to connect to these men (Greek "to them") with the verb "to prove" (TEV "Show"), and not with our boasting.

The verse may be translated as follows:

Show these men that you love them. The churches that sent them will hear about it, and this will prove to them that our boast about you was true.

Chapter 9

SECTION HEADING

Help for Fellow Christians: "The Offering for the Needy Fellow Christians (in Judea)."

In this chapter Paul gives final instructions about raising the offering for the needy fellow Christians in Judea (verses 1-5), and then speaks of how God blesses those who give generously to others (verses 6-15). Paul is still very careful in the way he makes his proposals, for he wants to avoid appearing to be giving orders to the people in Corinth. At the close of the chapter he speaks eloquently of the benefits that the offering will bring, not only to the needy Christians in Judea but also to the givers in Corinth, and to fellow believers elsewhere.

9.1   RSV   TEV
Now it is superfluous for me   There is really no need for
to write to you about the offer-   me to write you about the help
ing for the saints,   being sent to God's people in
                                      Judea.

superfluous: "unnecessary." The statement may be phrased thus: "I really don't need to write you" or "There is really no need for me to write you" (TEV). This is a polite disclaimer; Paul writes quite a bit about the subject. It might be better to translate "...for me to keep on writing you."

the offering for the saints: for the saints see 1.1; and for the whole phrase see 8.4. TEV makes explicit who the recipients are: "the help being sent to God's people in Judea." Or, "the offering being raised for our fellow Christians in Judea."

9.2   RSV   TEV
for I know your readiness, of which   I know that you are willing to
I boast about you to the people of   help, and I have boasted of you
Macedonia, saying that Achaia has   to the people in Macedonia. "The
been ready since last year; and   brothers in Achaia," I said, "have
your zeal has stirred up most of   been ready to help since last
them.   year." Your eagerness has stirred
                                      up most of them.

your readiness: see 8.11,12.
I boast: see 1.14.

[95]

the people of Macedonia: or "our fellow believers in Macedonia" or "the churches in Macedonia." For Macedonia see 1.16. Paul is probably in Macedonia as he writes this letter (see introduction, "Translating Paul's Second Letter to the Corinthians").

saying that...: it seems better, with TEV, to have a direct quotation: "'The brothers in Achaia,' I said, 'have been ready to help since last year.'"

Instead of "The brothers in Achaia" (TEV) it would be better to say "Our fellow Christians in Achaia." Paul speaks of the province of Achaia (see 1.1), but is referring specifically to the Christians in Corinth, to whom he is writing this letter.

since last year: as in 8.10.

zeal: "eagerness" (TEV), "enthusiasm," "strong desire (to help)."

stirred up: in the sense of "stimulated," "encouraged"; "filled them with the ambition to do the same."

most of them: or, perhaps, "all of them."

9.3	RSV	TEV
	But I am sending the brethren so that our boasting about you may not prove vain in this case, so that you may be ready, as I said you would be;	Now I am sending these brothers, so that our boasting about you in this matter may not turn out to be empty words. But, just as I said, you will be ready with your help.

the brethren: Titus and his two unnamed companions (see 8.23).

our boasting about you may not prove vain in this case: Paul sends the three men to make sure that the Corinthians will raise the offering and have it ready when he arrives (verses 4-5). In this way his boast about the Corinthians' generosity will be confirmed.

may not prove vain: "will not turn out to be a lie," "will not be shown to be an empty boast." Instead of the two negatives, a positive expression may be used: "will be proven true," "will be shown to be correct."

in this case: that is, in this specific matter of raising the offering.

as I said you would be: "as I told the Macedonian Christians you would be."

The verse may be translated as follows:
So I am sending these three Christian brothers to you, so that our boast about you in this matter will be justified (or, will turn out to be true). As I keep telling the Macedonians, you will be ready.

9.4	RSV	TEV
	lest if some Macedonians come with me and find that you are not ready, we be humiliated—to say nothing of you—for being so confident.	However, if the people from Macedonia should come with me and find out that you are not ready, how ashamed we would be—not to speak of your shame—for feeling so sure of you!

Paul points out that if the Corinthians do not have the offering ready when he and his Macedonian fellow believers arrive, then he will be ashamed. But, he adds tactfully, the Corinthians themselves will be ashamed—and Paul wants to avoid this.

It is better, with TEV, to begin a new sentence here; the construction lest...we be humiliated is very difficult for many English-speaking readers and should not be imitated. "For if some of our fellow Christians of Macedonia come with me and they discover that you do not have the offering ready, how ashamed we (or, I) will be!"

humiliated: or "embarrassed." This is a situation often aptly described by the vivid phrase "to lose face," for which many appropriate expressions exist in other languages.

to say nothing of you: this well represents the tactful way Paul impresses on his readers their loss of face. Or else, "I need not speak of your shame (or, embarrassment)."

It might be difficult to separate for being so confident from the verbal phrase we be humiliated, as RSV does (see also TEV). So it may be better to restructure as follows:

For when I arrive there with some fellow Christians from Macedonia, I do not want them to discover that you do not have the offering ready. If this happens, how embarrassed I will be for having been so sure about you! I need not add that you will be embarrassed also.

9.5	RSV	TEV
	So I thought it necessary to urge the brethren to go on to you before me, and arrange in advance for this gift you have promised, so that it may be ready not as an exaction but as a willing gift.	So I thought it was necessary to urge these brothers to go to you ahead of me and get ready in advance the gift you promised to make. Then it will be ready when I arrive, and it will show that you give because you want to, not because you have to.

I thought it necessary: or "I think it is necessary." Paul here uses the past tense of the verb from the point of view of the readers; that is, when they read the letter, Paul's thinking will be a past event. As he writes it, Paul is thinking that it is necessary to send Titus and the two other men.

the brethren: as in verse 3.

arrange in advance: "get ready before I arrive."

this gift you have promised: in Greek the word translated gift often means "blessing," that is, something that benefits or does good to someone.

The rest of the verse is a final clause in Greek, which is how RSV has translated it. It is better, however, to have a complete sentence, beginning with "In this way" or "Then," or something similar.

not as an exaction but as a willing gift: "not as something you were forced to do but as something you really wanted to do." The word translated exaction has the meaning of "greed," "avarice," and here characterizes the spirit of a selfish, greedy person who gives only because he is forced to do so.

9.5

The last part of the verse may be translated as follows: "In this way, the offering will be ready when I arrive. It will be given freely, instead of being forced out of you." Or, "You will give it because you want to, and not because you are forced to do so."

9.6	RSV	TEV
	The point is this; he who sows sparingly will also reap sparingly, and he who sows bountifully will also reap bountifully.	Remember that the person who plants few seeds will have a small crop; the one who plants many seeds will have a large crop.

The point is this: "This is what I mean." Paul cites the words that follow in order to illustrate what he means about the difference between a gift given freely and a forced contribution.

sows...reap: "plants seeds...gathers a harvest." The most general and widely known terms for planting and reaping should be used.

sparingly...bountifully: "little...much," "small...large." If verbal phrases such as "plant seeds" and "reap a harvest" are used, the same adjectives may not be natural for both actions; "plant a few seeds ...reap a small harvest; plant many seeds...reap a large harvest."

9.7	RSV	TEV
	Each one must do as he has made up his mind, not reluctantly or under compulsion, for God loves a cheerful giver.	Each one should give, then, as he has decided, not with regret or out of a sense of duty; for God loves the one who gives gladly.

do as he has made up his mind: "must give as he (himself) has decided." The verbal phrase made up his mind translates the Greek "purposed in his heart." This is a decision that comes from within a person, not one that is imposed from the outside.

reluctantly: "regretfully," or "sadly."

under compulsion: "is forced to do so."

The sentence structure favors the two negative expressions; but it is possible to use positive expressions: "cheerfully and willingly," "gladly and freely."

The last part of the verse is a free quotation from the ancient Greek version (the Septuagint) of Proverbs 22.8: "God blesses a generous and happy man."

a cheerful giver: "a person who is happy to give," "a person who gives gladly."

The following may serve as a model for the translation of this verse:

Each person should give as he (himself) has decided; but he should give cheerfully and willingly, because it is the person who gives gladly that God loves.

9.8 RSV	TEV
And God is able to provide you with every blessing in abundance, so that you may always have enough of everything and may provide in abundance for every good work.	And God is able to give you more than you need, so that you will always have all you need for yourselves and more than enough for every good cause.

provide you with every blessing in abundance: "bless you with far more gifts than you need," "give you all sorts of blessings in great abundance." God is both rich and generous, and he generously gives blessings of all kinds. Here you is plural.

enough of everything: Paul is talking about material as well as spiritual blessings. To generous people God gives all they need for themselves.

provide in abundance for every good work: "give generously to every good cause." Not only do generous people have enough for their own needs; they also have enough to contribute generously to good causes.

In Greek the statement about a generous giver having all he needs is a participial clause, so that it is subordinate to the statement about the capacity to give generously. That capacity is stated by a finite form of the verb "to abound." Strictly speaking the two are not parallel and perhaps a more accurate translation would be "...so that as your own needs are satisfied in every way, you will give generously to every good cause" or "...you will have more than enough to do all kinds of good works."

9.9 RSV	TEV
As it is written, "He scatters abroad, he gives to the poor; his righteousness^k endures for ever."	As the scripture says, "He gives generously to the needy; his kindness lasts forever."

^{k}Or benevolence

As it is written: "As the scripture says" (TEV). The text quoted is from Psalm 112.9, a passage which speaks of a righteous man, a man who does God's will.

The first line is composed of two statements, as RSV shows: He scatters abroad, he gives to the poor. The sense is "He gives generously to the poor" (see TEV). Since in the context of this verse God is the last one referred to by the third person singular (verse 8), the reader might be led to think that "He gives" refers to God. So it may be necessary to say "A good person gives generously to the poor."

righteousness: as the RSV footnote shows, the meaning here may be "kindness," "generosity," "openheartedness." This is the meaning preferred by most modern translations.

endures for ever: "never stops," "lasts forever" (TEV). But the text may be understood to mean "is never forgotten (by God)." That is, it may mean "God will remember his goodness, and reward him forever."

9.10 RSV	TEV
He who supplies seed to the sower and bread for food will supply and multiply your resources*l* and increase the harvest of your righteousness.*k*	And God, who supplies seed for the sower and bread to eat, will also supply you with all the seed you need and will make it grow and produce a rich harvest from your generosity.

*k*Or *benevolence*

*l*Greek *sowing*

In compressed language and rather dense constructions, Paul enlarges upon what he said in verse 8.

He who supplies seed to the sower and bread for food: this refers to God, and it is better to make this explicit: "And God, who supplies ...." The language is taken from Isaiah 55.10, where the prophet describes how the rain and snow that fall on fertile soil make it produce its crops, thereby providing seed for the sower and food to eat. Paul's words may be describing the whole process of planting the seed, harvesting the grain, and making the bread.

bread for food: "bread to eat" (TEV) or "food to eat."

will supply and multiply your resources: as the RSV footnote shows, the word translated resources is literally "(the act of) sowing." TEV expresses this with the phrase "will also supply you with all the seed you need"; or else, "...all the seed you can plant." This is a figure, of course, for the good deeds the readers are to perform—specifically, the offerings for needy fellow Christians.

multiply...and increase: TEV takes the two verbs to be quite close in meaning in this context, taking the first one ("to enlarge," "to make bigger") to describe what is implied by planting, namely, plants; it takes the second verb ("make grow") to describe the harvest. So, "will make it grow (or, will make the plants grow) and produce a rich harvest."

of your righteousness: again the meaning "generosity" (TEV) is preferable. As these last words make clear, Paul is saying that God uses human generosity to produce a rich harvest of good things for others. It is in the context of generous giving to needy fellow Christians that Paul is writing these words.

The verse may be translated as follows:

God is the one who gives seed for a man to sow, and gives him food to eat. So God will supply you with all the seed that you can plant, and will make the plants grow. And in this way he will make your generosity produce a large harvest.

9.11 RSV	TEV
You will be enriched in every way for great generosity, which through us will produce thanksgiving to God;	He will always make you rich enough to be generous at all times, so that many will thank God for your gifts which they receive from us.

You will be enriched: "God will make you rich."

for great generosity: that is, "so that you can be very generous." As TEV has it, "He will always make you rich enough to be generous at all times."

which through us: here Paul is speaking of the role that he and his companions will play. They will take the offering to the needy fellow Christians in Judea, and the Jewish Christians, in turn, will give thanksgiving to God. It is better to use verbal phrases as TEV does: "so that many people will thank God for your gifts which they receive from us."

9.12

RSV	TEV
for the rendering of this service not only supplies the wants of the saints but also overflows in many thanksgivings to God.	For this service you perform not only meets the needs of God's people, but also produces an outpouring of gratitude to God.

the rendering of this service: "this service you render," "this work you perform." The word translated service is used most often in the sense of a religious service, an act of worship. In Romans 15.27 the related verb is used of this very same offering.

not only supplies...but also overflows: "supplies...and overflows," "both supplies...and also overflows."

the wants of the saints: "the need of your (or, our) fellow believers."

overflows in many thanksgivings to God: "produces an abundance of grateful prayers (or, prayers of thanks) to God," "makes many people offer prayers of thanksgiving to God."

9.13

RSV	TEV
Under the test of this service, you^m will glorify God by your obedience in acknowledging the gospel of Christ, and by the generosity of your contribution for them and for all others;	And because of the proof which this service of yours brings, many will give glory to God for your loyalty to the gospel of Christ, which you profess, and for your generosity in sharing with them and everyone else.

^{m}Or they

Under the test of this service: "As a result of the proof that this service gives." RSV the test is an inadequate translation of the Greek; what is in focus is not the process of testing but the result, the proof, the demonstration of the Corinthians' spirit of Christian generosity.

you will glorify God: while this is possible, it is much better to follow the translation proposed in the RSV footnote, "they will glorify God," that is, the Jewish Christians, who will receive the gift, will give glory to God.

by your obedience: better, "for your obedience" or "for your loyalty" (TEV).

[101]

your obedience in acknowledging the gospel of Christ: this does
not make much sense; it is better to say "the obedience which characterizes (or, accompanies) your confession of the gospel of Christ." Or
else, "by the way you profess and obey the gospel of Christ."
the gospel of Christ: "the Good News about Christ."
by the generosity of your contribution for them and for all others:
"by how generous you were in sharing with (or, giving to) them and with
(or, to) everyone else."
The verse may be translated as follows:
For this service of yours will prove your Christian spirit,
and your fellow Christians will praise God for the way you
confess and obey the gospel of Christ. They will also praise
God for the generous way in which you have shared what you
have with them and with all other fellow believers.

9.14	RSV	TEV
	while they long for you and pray for you, because of the surpassing grace of God in you.	And so with deep affection they will pray for you because of the extraordinary grace God has shown you.

they long for you and pray for you: "with deep gratitude they will
pray for you." The offering will serve not only to meet the physical
needs of the Jewish Christians, but also to bring them into a sense of
fellowship and unity with the Gentile Christians.
surpassing grace of God in you: for grace of God see 1.12. Here
in you means "which you demonstrate," "which you show." But it seems
more faithful to translate "grace...upon you," that is, the great love
that God has shown the Corinthians.
The following may serve as a model for translating this verse:
With deep affection for you they will pray for you, because
of the extraordinary love which God has shown for you.

9.15	RSV	TEV
	Thanks be to God for his inexpressible gift!	Let us thank God for his priceless gift!

Thanks be to God: see 8.16.
inexpressible gift: that is, a gift which words cannot describe.
Various superlative expressions may serve: incomparable, unsurpassable,
indescribable. This is the gift of salvation, or of God's Son, by whom
we are saved.
The verse may be translated:
Let us thank God for his gift to us, a gift which words
cannot describe.

Chapter 10

Paul Defends His Ministry: "Paul's Authority as an Apostle,"
"Paul Asserts His Authority."

It has long been noticed that in chapters 10-13 the subject and
the tone of the letter change dramatically. In these four chapters Paul
strongly defends his ministry and sternly asserts his authority as an
apostle. The tone is caustic, not to say angry. He denounces his opponents and warns them that when he returns to Corinth he will deal
harshly with them.

Some scholars believe that these last four chapters were not written at the same time that the rest of the letter was written, but were
written earlier and are, in fact, the harsh letter (or, a part of it)
that Paul refers to in 2.3,4; 7.8,12. Whatever the case may be, it is
obvious that Paul is in a different state of mind as he writes (or
dictates) these chapters. He boldly affirms his authority and demands
that the Corinthian Christians follow his instructions.

In this section the first person plural is used most of the time,
but at times there is an abrupt change to the first person singular.
As noted earlier, the plural form may indicate that Paul is speaking
about himself and his companions, but it may simply be a conventional
way of speaking about himself. Some translations use the singular form
consistently in this section, and a translator should feel free to do
the same.

10.1 RSV	TEV
I, Paul, myself entreat you, by the meekness and gentleness of Christ—I who am humble when face to face with you, but bold to you when I am away!—	I, Paul, make a personal ap- peal to you—I who am said to be meek and mild when I am with you, but harsh with you when I am away. By the gentleness and kindness of Christ

Paul begins with an emphatic expression: I, Paul, myself entreat
you. The myself is strong. "It is I, Paul, who appeals to you," "I
myself make this personal appeal."

entreat: "beg," "appeal"; or "exhort," "urge."

by the meekness and gentleness of Christ: Paul bases his appeal
on Christ's own qualities of meekness and gentleness. It may be difficult to express the idea of urging by Christ's qualities. Paul wants
to be like Christ was, and it is in this spirit that he makes his appeal: "Christ was meek and gentle. Because of this, I beg you...."

meekness and gentleness: the two words are very close in meaning:
"kindness and gentleness," "reasonableness and patience."

I who am humble...but bold: RSV takes these words as Paul's own
description of himself. TEV and other translations, however, take them
to be what Paul's opponents say about him, and this seems better (see
verse 10, below). TEV has "meek and mild...harsh"; or else "timid...
arrogant," "afraid...brave."

RSV interrupts the sequence of the sentence by placing within
dashes what people say about Paul. This may not be the best way to
handle the matter. TEV changes the order of some of the expressions in
the verse, but still uses a dash to show an interruption. In many languages it will be better to do as follows: "I, Paul, now make a personal
appeal to you. It is said (or, People say) that when I am with you I am
timid, but when I am away I am bold." And then the verse can continue:
"I want to be as gentle and kind as Christ was. And so I beg you...."

(It should be noticed that in some editions of TEV the verse
number "2" is in the wrong place; instead of coming after "I beg you"
it should come before.)

10.2   RSV   TEV

I beg of you that when I am present   I beg you not to force me to be
I may not have to show boldness   harsh when I come; for I am sure
with such confidence as I count on   I can deal harshly with those who
showing against some who suspect   say that we act from worldly
us of acting in worldly fashion.   motives.

I beg of you that...I may not have to: Paul is asking that they
change their attitude so that he may be able to change his. He doesn't
want to be harsh or bold, as he now thinks he will have to be. "I beg
you not to force me to be harsh (or, stern) when I arrive there (or,
when I am present with you)."

show boldness with...confidence: here in the sense of being harsh,
stern, authoritarian.

as I count on showing: "as I intend to show," "as I am sure I can
be."

suspect us: here it is better to translate "accuse us," "allege
that we," "say (or, think) that we."

acting in worldly fashion: this translates the Greek phrase "walk-
ing according to the flesh" (see 1.17). Other possibilities are "act
from worldly motives" (TEV), "act from purely human motives," or even
"act as non-Christians." To live "according to the flesh" means to have
the attitude of people who do not submit to God's will in Christ, and
to live like them. So something like "unprincipled behavior" or "lack
of Christian principles" may be said. A word like "immoral" should not
be used if it implies sexual misconduct. Since in the next verse Paul
is going to make a play on the phrases "in the flesh" and "according
to the flesh," it is better to use the adjective "worldly" here, if
possible, as RSV and TEV do.

The following may serve as a model for translating this verse:
I beg you: don't force me to be harsh and stern when I arrive
there! I know I can be harsh with the people there who accuse
me of acting from worldly (or, unchristian) motives.

10.3   RSV   TEV
For though we live in the world   It is true that we live in the
we are not carrying on a worldly   world, but we do not fight from
war,   worldly motives.

   we live in the world: or, if the adjective "unchristian" is used
above, "we live in an unchristian world."
   we are not carrying on a worldly war: "we do not use worldly tac-
tics when we fight"; or "we do not fight from unchristian motives."
Here the word war is used in a figurative sense of the Christian's life
as a constant struggle against the forces of evil. In most languages
the metaphor can be used; but if it is not suitable, something like
a simile may be better: "we do not, as it were, fight from worldly
motives." If the simple figure is altogether inappropriate, it may have
to be modified: "our fight against (the forces of) evil is not carried
on from worldly motives." Or else, dropping the language of war altogether, "we are not ruled by worldly motives in our Christian life."

10.4   RSV   TEV
for the weapons of our warfare are The weapons we use in our fight
not worldly but have divine power   are not the world's weapons but
to destroy strongholds.   God's powerful weapons, which we
                                    use to destroy strongholds. We
                                    destroy false arguments;

   the weapons of our warfare are not worldly: here worldly translates the Greek adjective "carnal" or "fleshly." The same word or
phrase should be used here that is used for the translation of "flesh"
in verses 2-3.
   have divine power: "are the power of God," "God's powerful weapons" (TEV), "the weapons that God gives us."
   destroy strongholds: Paul continues with the figure of a war; and
strongholds ("fortresses," "strongly armed camps") may be represented
by "enemy strongholds," "strongholds of evil." But if such a concept
is difficult or impossible to portray, something like "defeat the
forces of evil" or "overcome the enemy forces" may be said.

10.5   RSV   TEV
We destroy arguments and every   we pull down every proud obstacle
proud obstacle to the knowledge   that is raised against the knowl-
of God, and take every thought   edge of God; we take every thought
captive to obey Christ,   captive and make it obey Christ.

   It is to be noticed that in the Greek text followed by TEV, "We
destroy false arguments" comes at the end of verse 4, not at the beginning of verse 5 as in the text translated by RSV.
   In this verse Paul defines what he means by the enemy's strongholds.
They are arguments and every proud obstacle to the knowledge of God. It
may be that Paul has only one idea in mind, that is, "all false arguments
that oppose themselves arrogantly to the knowledge of God." But if two
separate items are meant, arguments are "false arguments," "false ways

or reasoning." And every proud obstacle may be represented by "every obstacle (or, opposition) that proud (or, arrogant) people raise against the knowledge of God." The word translated obstacle means a high place, a fortified height, which is easy to defend and difficult to conquer. Here the knowledge of God means human knowledge about God; this must be stated explicitly, as in the following model for translating this part of the verse (following the verse division of TEV): "We destroy all false arguments, 5 and overcome every objection that proud people raise against the true knowledge about God." From Paul's point of view it is the gospel that brings to humankind the true knowledge about God.

and take every thought captive to obey Christ: here human thoughts are described as enemy soldiers which are captured in war. If this figure is hard to represent ("we capture every thought and make it obey Christ"), then a more simple expression may be used: "we (try to) make people think thoughts that are pleasing to Christ" or "we (try to) change people's minds so that their thinking is in accordance with Christ's demands."

10.6	RSV	TEV
	being ready to punish every diso-bedience, when your obedience is complete.	And after you have proved your complete loyalty, we will be ready to punish any act of dis-loyalty.

Here Paul speaks directly of the situation in Corinth, where there is active opposition to him in the church. It is better, with TEV, to make a full stop at the end of verse 5 and begin a new sentence here.

being ready to punish: "We are (or, I am) ready to punish."

every disobedience: "every disobedient action" or "every disobedient person."

when your obedience is complete: "as soon as we know that you are completely obedient." Paul is talking about obedience to himself (or, to himself and his companions), and it may be necessary to make this quite explicit. The more general idea of disobedience to God, rather than to Paul, might be intended; but in this instance Paul considers the two to be the same. Perhaps the following may serve as a model for translating this verse:

And as soon as you show that you are completely loyal (or, obedient) to us (or, to me), we are (or, I am) ready to punish anyone who is disloyal (or, disobedient).

10.7	RSV	TEV
	Look at what is before your eyes. If any one is confident that he is Christ's, let him remind himself that as he is Christ's, so are we.	You are looking at the out-ward appearance of things. Is there someone there who reckons himself to belong to Christ? Well, let him think again about himself, because we belong to Christ just as much as he does.

The first sentence in this verse may be understood as a statement, or as a command, or as a question. Most translations have either a command (as RSV does) or a statement (TEV). It is difficult to decide between the two: "Look at the plain facts" or "You consider only the outward appearance of things." There is no decisive argument for either alternative; perhaps the second one is favored by the words that follow, in which Paul speaks about his opponents in the church at Corinth.

If any one is confident that he is Christ's: as often, the conditional form does not express doubt but is a way of stating a fact. "The person (there) who is sure that he is Christ's servant (or, that he serves Christ)." TEV's question form may be imitated, if it is clear that Paul is not asking for information: "Does someone there feel certain that he is Christ's representative (or, that he represents Christ)?"

is Christ's: "belongs to Christ," "is Christ's servant," "is Christ's spokesman," "represents Christ," "has Christ's authority." The unnamed person's claim is that he has a special relationship to Christ which gives him more authority than anyone else's, including Paul's.

Paul tells that person to consider the fact that he, Paul, and his companions have the same kind of relationship to Christ which that man claims. Here Paul is obviously speaking about himself, and it may be better to translate by the singular "so am I" instead of so are we.

The verse may be translated as follows:

You are very superficial in your thinking. Someone there claims that he is the authorized spokesman for Christ. That man should think again, and he will realize that I am just as much a spokesman for Christ as he is.

10.8 RSV	TEV
For even if I boast a little too much of our authority, which the Lord gave for building you up and not for destroying you, I shall not be put to shame.	For I am not ashamed, even if I have boasted somewhat too much about the authority that the Lord has given us—authority to build you up, not to tear you down.

even if I boast a little too much: for boast see 1.12. Here boast is something one should not do. (Note that from 10.8 to 12.9 words meaning "boast" or "boastful" are used nineteen times.)

a little too much: this could be "a little more than my opponent does"; but it probably means "a little more than I should." Although expressed as a probability (even if), Paul is admitting that, in fact, he has boasted more than he should.

It seems better, with TEV, to start the sentence with "For I am not ashamed," so as to bring it into close relationship to the admission about boasting too much. Instead of TEV present tense "I am not ashamed," RSV has the future tense I shall not be put to shame, which is the tense used in Greek. The meaning would be that in some future encounter Paul will not be bested; his claim to authority will be upheld. But the future could be taken more generally to mean, "I have done nothing for which I should be ashamed"; and other translations, like TEV, use the present tense. The shame here is that of losing face, of being embarrassed, should his claims to authority be proven false (see 9.4).

our authority, which the Lord gave for building you up and not for destroying you: the authority which Paul has received from the Lord Jesus Christ is to be used for constructive, not destructive, purposes. He is to help the Corinthians become better Christians in every way; he should encourage them and support them at all times.

The verse may be translated as follows:

The Lord Jesus Christ has given us (or, me) authority over you, not to tear you down (or, destroy you), but to build you up. And even though I have boasted a little too much about our (or, my) authority, I have nothing to be ashamed of.

10.9	RSV	TEV
	I would not seem to be frightening you with letters.	I do not want it to appear that I am trying to frighten you with my letters.

I would not seem: "I don't want to appear," "I don't want you to think of me." Implied here is an explanation: "I won't say more than this, because I do not want to appear...."

frightening you: the verb is a strong one, appearing only here in the New Testament: the related adjective appears twice (Mark 9.6; Heb 12.21). A strong verb such as "terrify" would be better.

with letters: "with my letters" (TEV). As he writes this; there have been at least two letters: what we know as 1 Corinthians, and the one before that, referred to in 1 Corinthians 5.9.

10.10	RSV	TEV
	For they say, "His letters are weighty and strong, but his bodily presence is weak, and his speech of no account."	Someone will say, "Paul's letters are severe and strong, but when he is with us in person, he is weak, and his words are nothing!"

For they say: "People say"; or "Someone says." TEV "Someone will say" takes the Greek to mean that Paul is arguing against what people might say. It is better to follow RSV here.

His letters are weighty and strong: "Paul's letters are strict and stern" or "...harsh and demanding." It may be necessary to characterize the contents of the letters and not the letters as such: "He writes harsh and demanding things in his letters."

his bodily presence is weak: "he is physically unimpressive," "when he is with us he doesn't impress anyone," "in person he is not impressive." The words are not so much a statement about Paul's looks as they are about the effect he had by his mere presence, how people reacted when they saw him in person.

his speech of no account: this refers to his ability as a public speaker: "he doesn't know how to speak," "as an orator he is nothing."

10.11　　　　RSV	TEV
Let such people understand that what we say by letter when absent, we do when present.	Such a person must understand that there is no difference between what we write in our letters when we are away and what we will do when we are there with you.

Let such people understand: it is to be noticed that here (and in verse 10) TEV has the singular, "Such a person must understand." The form in Greek in verses 10 and 11 is singular, but it may be a way of speaking about people in general, and not someone in particular. A translator is free to choose either the singular or the plural.

what we say by letter when absent, we do when present: Paul says his actions match his words. He will be just as decisive and demanding when he deals personally with the troubles in Corinth as he is when he writes about them. There are several ways to say this: "when I am there in Corinth, my attitude will be exactly the same it is in the letter that I write you while I am away from you"; "my attitude as I write you this letter, while I am absent from you, is no different from the attitude I will take when I arrive there." TEV provides another way to translate the verse.

10.12　　　　RSV	TEV
Not that we venture to class or compare ourselves with some of those who commend themselves. But when they measure themselves by one another, and compare themselves with one another, they are without understanding.	Of course we would not dare classify ourselves or compare ourselves with those who rate themselves so highly. How stupid they are! They make up their own standards to measure themselves by, and they judge themselves by their own standards!

RSV places this verse as the last one in the paragraph; TEV begins a new paragraph with it. Most modern translations are like TEV.

Here Paul speaks directly about his opponents, the false apostles (11.4-5). With heavy sarcasm he affirms that of course he doesn't measure up to their standards, since they make their standards to fit themselves. So when they measure themselves by those standards, they find that they are ideal Christians! Paul will have nothing to do with such nonsense.

Not that we venture: it is better to begin verse 12 with a definite break from verse 11, as TEV does: "Of course we would not dare...." TEV tries to bring out the sarcasm in Paul's words.

to class or compare ourselves with: there is a play on words in Greek, which in English may be represented by "to pair ourselves or compare ourselves with." The first verb means "to classify (among)." Here "to class ourselves with" means to include ourselves in the same classification with the others. The second verb means "to compare": "compare ourselves with" those other people.

who commend themselves: for the verb see 3.1, the passage which speaks of letters of recommendation; "who praise themselves," "who write their own letters of recommendation."

measure themselves...and compare themselves: the process is that
of people who draw up their own standards by which to measure excellence. But their standards are made to fit their own qualities, so that
when they measure themselves they are perfect. TEV tries to bring out
the meaning: "They make up their own standards to measure themselves by,
and they judge themselves by their own standards!" Or, "They make their
own standard to fit themselves, and then measure themselves by it."

they are without understanding: this is a bit weak; it is better
to say "they are fools," "they are being stupid," "they are acting
senselessly." Or else the statement can be worked in with the second
sentence in the verse, as follows: "Those stupid (or, foolish) people
draw up standards to fit themselves, and then measure themselves by
those standards!"

10.13	RSV	TEV
	But we will not boast beyond limit, but will keep to the limits God has apportioned us, to reach even to you.	As for us, however, our boasting will not go beyond certain limits; it will stay within the limits of the work which God has set for us, and this includes our work among you.

In contrast with his opponents, Paul and his companions will keep
within the limits that God has set for them, and will not make any
claims that go beyond those limits. The Corinthians themselves are included within the area that God assigned to Paul and his companions;
his opponents, Paul implies, are intruders. They have no right to be
there.

we will not boast beyond limit: the limit Paul speaks of is the
one set by God. There is a proper, Christian basis for pride, but there
is also excessive pride that is not proper. "Our (or, My) boasting, however, will not go beyond the proper limits; it will stay within the
limits of the work that God set for us (or, for me)." It is to be remembered that the first plural we and us may be rendered "I" and "me,"
as references to Paul alone.

to reach even to you: "and you are included within those limits."
That is, Corinth was part of the territory that God had assigned to
Paul and his companions. Paul was not transgressing when he worked in
Corinth; by implication, his opponents were.

10.14	RSV	TEV
	For we are not overextending our-selves, as though we did not reach you; we were the first to come all the way to you with the gospel of Christ.	And since you are within those limits, we were not going beyond them when we came to you, bringing the Good News about Christ.

The first part of the verse in RSV is unintelligible. Paul is saying that in going to Corinth he was not going beyond the proper limits

that God had set, as would be the case if those limits did not include
Corinth. "Since you are included within the limits that God set for us
(or, for me), we (or, I) did not go beyond them when we (or, I) went
to Corinth."

we were the first to come all the way to you: the Greek verb may
mean "to come first." In this case Paul would be making the point that
he did not go to places where others had started the Christian work.
But here it is more likely that the verb means simply "to come," "to
arrive," as TEV translates.

with the gospel of Christ: "proclaiming the Good News about
Christ."

The verse may be translated as follows:
You are included within the area that God has assigned to me,
and so I did not go beyond my limit when I went all the way to
Corinth to proclaim the Good News about Christ.

10.15 RSV	TEV
We do not boast beyond limit, in other men's labors; but our hope is that as your faith increases, our field among you may be greatly enlarged,	So we do not boast about the work that others have done beyond the limits God set for us. Instead, we hope that your faith may grow and that we may be able to do a much greater work among you, always within the limits that God has set.

We do not boast beyond limit, in other men's labors: it is difficult to tell what the Greek text means. The first part, translated by
RSV We do not boast beyond limit, is similar to the beginning of verse
13. But its meaning seems different, since it relates to what Paul has
just said in verse 14 about the Corinthians being within the limit that
God set for him. Paul seems to be saying that he does not, as his opponents do, boast about work that others have done outside the limit
which God has set for Paul himself. "So we do not boast of work that
others do (or, have done) outside the limit that God set for us."

our hope is: Paul clearly hopes that Corinth may not be the extreme limit of the area God has assigned him. He hopes that as the work
in Corinth prospers, it may spread even further west.

as your faith increases: or "that your faith will grow." By increase
of faith Paul is talking about the growth of effectiveness of the church
in Corinth. Once the dispute is settled, the church will be able to do
greater and more effective Christian work in the city of Corinth and
the whole province of Achaia.

our field among you may be greatly enlarged: while possible, this
does not seem an adequate translation of the Greek. It seems rather
that Paul is saying "our work among you will keep on growing" or, alter-
natively, "our influence among you will become even greater." And then
comes the qualifying phrase in Greek "according to our standard," which
means "according to the limit that God set for us." Paul clearly hopes
that his work in Corinth will now start growing again, but he is careful to state that he will not exceed the limits that God has set. The
hope of going beyond Corinth is clearly expressed in the next verse.

[111]

10.15

The second half of the verse may be translated as follows: "But we (or, I) hope that our (or, my) work there will extend itself greatly; of course we (or, I) will always stay within the limits that God has set."

10.16 RSV	TEV
so that we may preach the gospel in lands beyond you, without boasting of work already done in another's field.	Then we can preach the Good News in other countries beyond you and shall not have to boast about work already done in another man's field.

so that we may preach the gospel in lands beyond you: "and then we will be able to spread (or, proclaim) the Good News in countries beyond Corinth." Paul clearly considers that the limit that God has set for him does not stop at Corinth, but goes beyond. So he plans to go on further west, spreading the Good News in other parts of the Roman Empire.

without boasting: implied is the thought "as some people do." Paul is referring to his opponents in Corinth, whom he sees as intruders who are taking credit for the work that he himself had done there. He plans to go to places where the Good News has not yet been preached.

The verse may be translated as follows:
If this happens, we (or, I) will be able to go to countries beyond Corinth and proclaim the gospel. We will not take credit for work done by someone else in the place (or, area) assigned him (or, that God assigned him)."

10.17 RSV	TEV
"Let him who boasts, boast of the Lord."	But as the scripture says, "Whoever wants to boast must boast about what the Lord has done."

Paul quotes Jeremiah 9.24 without the introductory words as it is written (as he does in 1 Cor 1.31). RSV relies only on quotation marks; it is better to do as TEV has done, "But as the scripture says."

The translation of this quotation should be exactly the same as in 1 Corinthians 1.31.

10.18 RSV	TEV
For it is not the man who commends himself that is accepted, but the man whom the Lord commends.	For it is when the Lord thinks well of a person that he is really approved, and not when he thinks well of himself.

the man who commends himself: this is the same verb used in verse 12 (and see 3.1). The translation could be "who praises himself," "who speaks (or, thinks) highly of himself."

that is accepted: is Paul speaking of divine approval or human approval? It would be more in keeping with the context if he were referring to God's approval. But if the word is translated, as it is by some, "to be accepted," then it is human approval. On the whole, divine approval seems preferable. "God does not approve of people who praise themselves; rather, his approval is given to those whom he praises." Or, "God's approval does not come as a result of a person's self praise, but only of God's praise."

Chapter 11

Paul and the False Apostles: "Paul Accuses the False Leaders of
the Church in Corinth."

In this section Paul denounces his opponents in the church at
Corinth, calling them false apostles and liars who try to appear as
genuine apostles of Christ (verse 13). These are very harsh words,
indeed, and if these four chapters are part of the earlier harsh letter
that Paul had written, it is easy to see why the Corinthians were upset
and distressed.

Paul vigorously defends his own conduct from the accusations made
against him, and in particular he is anxious to establish that he has
not benefited financially from the church at Corinth (verses 7-10).

Paul's attitude as he wrote these angry words is different from
his attitude when he wrote the loving and conciliatory words of the
earlier part of the letter (chapters 1-9). Yet even here his deep love
for the Corinthians shows through (verse 11).

11.1 RSV	TEV
I wish you would bear with me in a little foolishness. Do bear with me!	I wish you would tolerate me, even when I am a bit foolish. Please do!

bear with me: "put up with me," "tolerate me," "allow me to be."
It is important to use a word here that will apply equally well to the
situation in verses 4 and 19-20, where Paul speaks of how the Corinthians put up with the false leaders.

in a little foolishness: that is, Paul is going to act like a
fool. Actually it is not until verse 16 that he starts talking like a
fool (see verse 20). The specific form of foolishness he refers to is the
boasting he will do. "Please put up with a bit of foolishness on my
part!" "I wish you would let me be a little foolish" or "...do a bit of
foolish boasting."

Do bear with me!: both RSV and TEV translate the Greek verb as a
command (TEV "Please do!"); but it may be read as an indicative: "But
of course you will put up with me!" On the whole the imperative seems
preferable.

11.2 RSV	TEV
I feel a divine jealousy for you, for I betrothed you to Christ to	I am jealous for you, just as God is; you are like a pure virgin

| present you as a pure bride to her one husband. | whom I have promised in marriage to one man only, Christ himself. |

In this verse Paul portrays himself as a father who is making arrangements for his daughter to get married.

I feel a divine jealousy: this translates the Greek "I am zealous (or, jealous) for you with God's zeal (or, jealousness)." In English there is a difference between "zealous" and "jealous"; "zealous" means to have an intense concern, and "jealous" means to be envious. But there is a sense in which jealousness is regarded as a virtue: for example, "he is jealous for his good name," "she is jealous for her reputation." Here it indicates an intense concern for a person's honor. So in English, at least, "I am jealous for you" (TEV) is an acceptable translation.

a divine jealousy: "with God's own jealousy," "with the jealousy that God gives me," or "as God is jealous." Paul claims his concern is the same as God's.

I betrothed: this refers to the formal agreement to marry; but at that time marriage itself would come later, as much as a year or more later. Here the marriage is referred to by to present you as a pure bride to her one husband. It is possible that Paul regards the present relationship between the church at Corinth (you) and Christ as a betrothal, an engagement; the wedding itself will come at the last day. Paul is deeply concerned for the Corinthians, trying his best to keep them completely devoted to Christ, so that at the wedding the bride will be a virgin.

to present you as a pure bride: better, "to present you, at the wedding, as a pure virgin."

to her one husband: or "to one man only." This may seem a bit odd, but Paul is emphasizing that Christ is the one man to whom the bride, the church at Corinth, has been promised in marriage; and she must remain faithful to him alone.

The following may serve as a model for the translation of this verse:

I have a deep concern for you; it is the same concern that God has. I arranged for your marriage to Christ, and I want you to remain pure, so that on the wedding day I can give you to him as a pure virgin to her husband.

This proposed translation assumes that it is possible, without further explanation, to use the figure of a bride, a groom, and the bride's father, to represent the church at Corinth, Christ, and the apostle Paul. But it may be necessary to do otherwise:

I have a very deep concern for you; I feel toward you as God does. I want you to remain completely faithful to Jesus Christ, just as a girl is faithful to the man she has promised to marry, and remains a virgin until the wedding day.

11.3	RSV	TEV
	But I am afraid that as the serpent deceived Eve by his cunning, your thoughts will be led astray	I am afraid that your minds will be corrupted and that you will abandon your full and pure devotion

| from a sincere and pure devotion to Christ. | to Christ—in the same way that Eve was deceived by the snake's clever lies. |

Paul uses the account in Genesis 3 as an illustration of what he is trying to prevent.

as the serpent deceived Eve by his cunning: "as the snake was cunning (or, clever) and deceived Eve," or "...and led Eve astray," or "...and caused Eve to sin."

your thoughts will be led astray: "your mind will be seduced," "your thinking will be corrupted." Paul probably thinks of the Devil as the one who will corrupt them.

a sincere and pure devotion to Christ: "a total and pure love for Christ."

The verse may be translated as follows: "I am afraid that what happened to Eve may happen to you. The snake was cunning, and he caused Eve to sin. In the same way your thinking may be corrupted, and you will no longer be completely faithful to Christ."

11.4 RSV	TEV
For if some one comes and preaches another Jesus than the one we preached, or if you receive a different spirit from the one you received, or if you accept a different gospel from the one you accepted, you submit to it readily enough.	For you gladly tolerate anyone who comes to you and preaches a different Jesus, not the one we preached; and you accept a spirit and a gospel completely different from the Spirit and the gospel you received from us!

Now Paul explains what he means by the Corinthians being seduced.

if some one comes: this is not a true conditional but a way of stating a fact. The concluding you submit to it readily enough should be translated "you gladly (or, willingly) put up with him." So it is better to do as TEV has done, and place this first: "you gladly tolerate anyone who comes...."

another Jesus...a different spirit...a different gospel: Paul does not specify what the differences are. For the first one: "and his message about Jesus is different from the message we proclaimed." It would not be, strictly speaking, a different Jesus as such, but a different message about him.

It is a bit more difficult to speak of if you receive a different spirit from the one you received. From Paul's point of view, what the Corinthians received when he proclaimed the gospel was the one true Holy Spirit. Perhaps: "and you receive (or, are offered) a spirit that is not the Holy Spirit, which you received from us." It is possible that Paul considered the spirit given by the false apostles to be satanic.

If you accept a different gospel: "and the gospel message you accept from him is different from the one you heard from us."

The verse may be translated as follows:

I am afraid for you because I see how easily (or, willingly) you tolerate those who come to you. You believe their message about Jesus even though it is different from the one I (or, we) preached! You accept the spirit they promise, which is not the Holy Spirit you received from me (or, us)! And you accept the gospel they proclaim, even though it is different from the one I (or, we) proclaimed!

11.5   **RSV**

I think that I am not in the least inferior to these superlative apostles.

TEV

I do not think that I am the least bit inferior to those very special so-called "apostles" of yours!

I think that: "But I am sure that," "I know that."

I am not in the least inferior: instead of the negative form, the positive equivalent might be more effective: "But I consider myself to be every bit as good as..." or "I think that I am the equal of...."

these superlative apostles: this is how Paul sarcastically describes them. It is from the Corinthians' point of view that they are superlative, "very superior," "superapostles," "extra special." TEV has "so-called 'apostles,'" since Paul does not regard them as true apostles. It might be better to say "these people you call the super-apostles" or "these people you regard as the greatest apostles."

11.6   **RSV**

Even if I am unskilled in speaking, I am not in knowledge; in every way we have made this plain to you in all things.

TEV

Perhaps I am an amateur in speaking, but certainly not in knowledge; we have made this clear to you at all times and in all conditions.

Even if: an admission that what follows is true. "It is true that," "I admit that," "Even though."

unskilled in speaking: "an amateur speaker," "a poor orator" (see 10.10). Paul admits the truth of this charge.

not in knowledge: that is, knowledge about the gospel (see 8.7).

in every way...in all things: "at all times...in all circumstances." The Corinthians knew, from personal experience, that Paul's knowledge of the gospel was profound and thorough.

11.7   **RSV**

Did I commit a sin in abasing myself so that you might be exalted, because I preached God's gospel without cost to you?

TEV

I did not charge you a thing when I preached the Good News of God to you; I humbled myself in order to make you important.

Paul goes to some length to establish the fact that he has not received financial aid from the Corinthians. This may have been one of the accusations made against him, which he is determined to refute.

The verse includes a statement about Paul's conduct and a sarcastic question prompted by that fact. RSV follows the order of the Greek literally, which makes for a long and complex question. It is better to divide and restructure as TEV has done.

Did I commit a sin...?: this is the question. "Did I do wrong?" "Was that a sin?" "Was that a bad thing?" This rhetorical question is, of course, sarcastic. "That was not a sin!" "I did nothing wrong!"

abasing myself so that you might be exalted: TEV "I humbled myself in order to make you important." It is not quite clear what Paul means by this. Probably "I humbled myself" refers to his habit of working to support himself wherever he went (for Corinth, see Acts 18.3; elsewhere: 1 Thes 2.9; Acts 20.33-35). Or else he might be referring specifically to the sufferings and persecutions he endured in his work (see 1 Cor 4.11-13). The "exaltation" of the Corinthians, in contrast with Paul's "abasement," may mean nothing more than that Paul was willing to be a servant so that the Corinthians might be helped. Or else the verb "to exalt," "to lift up," might have the theological sense of lifting up from a life of idolatry and sin.

I preached God's gospel without cost to you: this is the statement of fact. It is to be noticed that here Paul uses the singular form I, not the plural "we."

God's gospel: "the Good News that comes from God," "the Good News of how God saves us," "the message of salvation."

without cost to you: "without charging you anything," "and I didn't charge you for it."

The verse may be translated as follows:

I proclaimed the divine message of salvation to you, and did not charge you anything. I took an inferior place (or, I had less) so that you might be raised to a superior place (or, so that you might have more). Was that a sin on my part?

11.8	RSV	TEV
	I robbed other churches by accepting support from them in order to serve you.	While I was working among you, I was paid by other churches. I was robbing them, so to speak, in order to help you.

I robbed other churches: Paul explains immediately what he means. He was helped financially by other churches in order to be able to do his work among the Corinthians without charging anything. To make clear that Paul is being ironic, TEV has "I was robbing them, so to speak." Or else, "I exploited other churches," "I took advantage of other churches."

to serve: in the Christian sense, working to spread the gospel and to help the church.

The following may serve as a model for translating this verse:
I received money from other churches to do my work among you. I could say that I robbed them in order to help you.

11.9   RSV   TEV
And when I was with you and was in   And during the time I was with
want, I did not burden any one,   you I did not bother you for help
for my needs were supplied by the   when I needed money; the brothers
brethren who came from Macedonia.   who came from Macedonia brought
So I refrained and will refrain   me everything I needed. As in the
from burdening you in any way.   past, so in the future: I will
                                        never be a burden to you!

and was in want: "and needed help," "and was in need," "and had
no money."
I did not burden any one: that is, "I did not impose on any of
you." The same verb is used in 12.13-14.
my needs were supplied by the brethren who came from Macedonia:
it is possible that the brethren were Timothy and Silas, whose arrival
from Macedonia while Paul was in Corinth is narrated in Acts 18.5. In
Philippians 4.14-20 Paul speaks gratefully of help that he had received
from the church in Philippi (which was in Macedonia).
I refrained and will refrain from burdening you: here a different
expression in Greek is used, but the meaning is the same, "to be a
financial burden."
The verse may be translated as follows:
During the time I was with you I needed financial help, but I
did not bother you for it (or, I did not impose on you). The
Christian brothers who arrived from Macedonia supplied me with
everything I needed. I did not impose on you then, and I will
not now or ever impose on you for help.

11.10   RSV   TEV
As the truth of Christ is in me,   By Christ's truth in me, I promise
this boast of mine shall not be   that this boast of mine will not
silenced in the regions of Achaia.   be silenced anywhere in all of
                                        Achaia.

As the truth of Christ is in me: this is in the form of an oath,
or a pledge, similar to the one in 10.1. By the truth of Christ Paul
means that what Christ was, said, and did was always true; and he,
Paul, is like Christ. "Christ always spoke the truth (or, was true),
and I do the same (or, am the same)."
this boast of mine shall not be silenced: "no one will be able to
keep me from boasting," "no person will ever stop me from making this
boast." Paul speaks the truth, and no one can deny it. For boast see
comments on 1.14.
the regions of Achaia: "everywhere in (the province of) Achaia."
For Achaia see 1.1.
The verse may be translated as follows:
Christ always spoke the truth, and I am doing the same when I
say that nobody in all of Achaia will be able to stop me from
making this boast (or, from boasting like this).

[119]

11.11 RSV	TEV
And why? Because I do not love you? God knows I do!	Do I say this because I don't love you? God knows I love you!

And why?: "Why do I say this?" or "Why do I boast like this?" or else, "Why do I act like this?"

In saying that the Corinthians had never helped him financially, Paul seems to be saying that they are ungrateful, stingy people, and that he doesn't care for them. Or else, in refusing to accept payment from Corinth, Paul appears to be saying he doesn't want to be under any obligation to them; that is, he refuses to treat them as friends. Of course Paul is their friend, and he loves them dearly.

11.12 RSV	TEV
And what I do I will continue to do, in order to undermine the claim of those who would like to claim that in their boasted mission they work on the same terms as we do.	I will go on doing what I am doing now, in order to keep those other "apostles" from having any reason for boasting and saying that they work in the same way that we do.

what I do I will continue to do: that is, his policy of not accepting help from the church in Corinth. Evidently the accusation made by Paul's opponents had hurt him very much.

to undermine the claim of those who: it is better at once to identify who are the people Paul refers to by the relative phrase those who. So TEV has "those other 'apostles'"; "apostles" is placed within quotation marks to show (as in verse 5) that Paul does not really consider them apostles at all (see the same expression in verse 5). The expression to undermine the claim of means "to take away the reason for," "to remove the opportunity of." The false leaders at Corinth claim they do their work as "apostles" in the same way that Paul does. Evidently they received pay from the church and were saying that Paul did the same. Paul vows never to receive pay from the Corinthian church, in order to deny those false leaders the opportunity of saying that they and Paul work on the same basis.

their boasted mission: "the work they boast about," "the boasts they make about their work."

on the same terms: "under the same conditions," "on the same basis." The verse may be translated as follows:

I will continue my policy of not accepting financial help from you. I want to prevent those so-called apostles from having any reason to claim that they work on the same basis that I (or, we) do.

11.13 RSV	TEV
For such men are false apostles, deceitful workmen, disguising themselves as apostles of Christ.	Those men are not true apostles— they are false apostles, who lie about their work and disguise themselves to look like real apostles of Christ.

false apostles: "they claim to be apostles but are not," "are not true apostles."

deceitful workmen: "they lie about their work," "dishonest workers."

disguising themselves as apostles of Christ: "making themselves look like apostles of Christ." The verb translated disguising is used again in verses 14,15, and the word chosen here should be appropriate for those two verses.

11.14	RSV	TEV
And no wonder, for even Satan disguises himself as an angel of light.		Well, no wonder! Even Satan can disguise himself to look like an angel of light!

no wonder: "that is not surprising," "there is nothing unusual about that"; or, in a positive form, "that is to be expected," "that is quite understandable."

Satan: see 2.11.

an angel of light: not "an angel made of light" but "a shining angel." Angels shone with the glory of God (see Luke 2.9).

11.15	RSV	TEV
So it is not strange if his servants also disguise themselves as servants of righteousness. Their end will correspond to their deeds.		So it is no great thing if his servants disguise themselves to look like servants of righteousness. In the end they will get exactly what their actions deserve.

is not strange: "is nothing to be surprised at," "is nothing unusual"; or in a positive form, "it is easy enough," "it is simple."

his servants: that is, Satan's servants, or helpers.

also disguise themselves as servants of righteousness: "also disguise themselves and appear to be servants of righteousness." Here, in contrast with Satan, righteousness is God's way, God's will; so the phrase may be "servants of the righteous God" or "servants of God, who is righteous (or, just)."

Their end will correspond to their deeds: "In the end they will be punished as they deserve." "Their final punishment (by God) will be exactly what their wicked actions deserve (or, what they deserve for their wicked actions)."

SECTION HEADING

Paul's Sufferings as an Apostle: "Paul Boasts about His Sufferings."

In this section Paul finally does the "foolish" boasting he talked about doing in verse 1. He admits it is foolishness (verse 21), but he must do it, and asks the Corinthians to be patient with him. He talks about his nationality (verse 22), about his hard work (verse 23a), and especially, and at length, about his sufferings and persecutions (verses 23b-33).

11.16 RSV	TEV
I repeat, let no one think me foolish; but even if you do, accept me as a fool, so that I too may boast a little.	I repeat: no one should think that I am a fool. But if you do, at least accept me as a fool, just so I will have a little to boast of.

I repeat: picking up from verse 1.
let no one think me foolish: "no one (of you) should think that I really am a fool."
even if you do: Paul admits that some will think he is a fool, and to them he says "at least accept me as a fool" (TEV). He deserves that much tolerance, or good will, from them.
I too may boast: "I also (as well as others) may boast." The implication is that his opponents, the false apostles, had started this business of boasting (see verse 18). But the Greek need not necessarily mean this, and it may mean, as TEV and others have it, "just so I will have a little to boast of."

11.17 RSV	TEV
(What I am saying I say not with the Lord's authority but as a fool, in this boastful confidence;	Of course what I am saying now is not what the Lord would have me say; in this matter of boasting I am really talking like a fool.

RSV places verses 17-18 within parentheses, since the thought goes directly from verse 16 to verse 19. In these two verses Paul explains why he must boast, even though it is not what the Lord Jesus Christ would have him do.
not with the Lord's authority but as a fool: "I am not following the Lord's advice (or, instructions) but am being (or, acting like) a fool."
in this boastful confidence: it seems better, with TEV, to translate "in this matter of boasting." The Greek word that RSV translates confidence means, in this context, "business (at hand)," "matter," "subject being discussed."
The verse may be translated as follows:
I am not following the Lord Jesus Christ's orders when I
boast like this; I am being a fool (or, acting foolishly).
TEV offers another possibility.

11.18 RSV	TEV
since many boast of worldly things, I too will boast.)	But since there are so many who boast for merely human reasons, I will do the same.

boast of worldly things: better "boast from worldly motives" (see the same phrase "according to the flesh" in 10.2-3). Or else, like TEV, translate "boast for merely human reasons." Paul feels forced to imitate those whose motives for boasting are not Christian. Here he goes against the scripture he quotes in 10.17.

11.19   RSV   TEV
For you gladly bear with fools,   You yourselves are so wise, and
being wise yourselves!   so you gladly tolerate fools!

With a plea for tolerance, practically an apology for what he is doing, Paul begins: "You yourselves are so wise, and so you gladly tolerate fools!" This being wise yourselves is said in irony (see 1 Cor 4.8). For bear with see verse 1.

11.20   RSV   TEV
For you bear it if a man makes   You tolerate anyone who orders
slaves of you, or preys upon you,   you around or takes advantage of
or takes advantage of you, or puts   you or traps you or looks down
on airs, or strikes you in the   on you or slaps you in the face.
face.

The Corinthians (again Paul is being sarcastic) put up with all sorts of abuse; surely they can put up with a bit of foolish boasting!
if a man: again this is more than a possibility; it is Paul's way of saying what had actually happened in Corinth. He is talking about the false apostles.
makes slaves of you: the false apostles had assumed complete domination over the Corinthian Christians and were ordering them around like slaves. They are not actual slaves, of course; they are treated as such. So it may be better to translate "treats you as slaves."
preys upon you: "takes advantage of you" (TEV), "exploits you," "uses you for his own purposes." Perhaps Paul is talking about financial exploitation.
takes advantage of you: TEV "traps you"; or else, "takes you in," "fools you." It is not clear, from the Greek verb Paul uses, exactly what he had in mind. In 12.16 the same verb is used with the meaning "to trap" (by guile).
puts on airs: "acts superior." TEV "looks down on you"; or else, "depises you."
strikes you in the face: it is doubtful that Paul is speaking of physical abuse; he probably means insulting behavior: "insults you," or even "curses you"; "treats you shamefully."

11.21   RSV   TEV
To my shame, I must say, we were   I am ashamed to admit that we
too weak for that!   were too timid to do those things!

    But whatever any one dares   But if anyone dares to boast
to boast of—I am speaking as a   about something—I am talking like
fool—I also dare to boast of that.   a fool—I will be just as daring.

With heavy sarcasm Paul says "I am ashamed to admit (or confess) that I was much too timid to do that!"

The verb we were...weak is not used in a literal sense: "we were (or, I was) not brave (or, bold) enough to do that!"

Both RSV and TEV begin a paragraph with the second half of verse 21, since now Paul begins to talk like a fool.

I am speaking as a fool (see verse 17): this is placed within dashes, as Paul interrupts himself to admit that what he proposes to do is a foolish thing. But it may be better to change the position of this admission, as follows: "I will now act like a fool and (will myself) boast of things other people boast about." Or, "Like a fool I am going to do what others do, and boast about the same things they do."

11.22 RSV	TEV
Are they Hebrews? So am I. Are they Israelites? So am I. Are they descendants of Abraham? So am I.	Are they Hebrews? So am I. Are they Israelites? So am I. Are they Abraham's descendants? So am I.

Hebrews: this refers primarily to race.

Israelites: that is, people of the covenant; this speaks primarily of religion.

descendants of Abraham: heirs to the promise that God made to Abraham. This emphasizes history and culture. The three do not have completely separate meanings, but refer to race, nationality, and religion in general.

The question form of the Greek is effective in English and should be imitated, if the same effect is achieved; that is, it shows that Paul's opponents have no advantage over Paul himself. But if the question and response pattern is not effective, it might be better to use a statement: "They (say they) are Hebrews—well, so am I! They (say they) are Israelites—I am one too! They (say they) are descendants of Abraham—well, so am I!" Or else, but with less effect, "I am just as much a Hebrew, an Israelite, and a descendant of Abraham as they are." "They boast about being Hebrews, Israelites, and descendants of Abraham; well, I can make the same boast!"

11.23 RSV	TEV
Are they servants of Christ? I am a better one—I am talking like a madman—with far greater labors, far more imprisonments, with countless beatings, and often near death.	Are they Christ's servants? I sound like a madman—but I am a better servant than they are! I have worked much harder, I have been in prison more times, I have been whipped much more, and I have been near death more often.

servants of Christ: here Paul does not say apostles (as in 11.13), but the more general term servants. He immediately responds, "I am a better servant!" qualifying this assertion by the admission that he sounds like a madman. This is stronger even than talking like a fool (verse 21). Paul sounds crazy when he claims to be a more dedicated

servant of Christ, but he will now prove his claim by reciting the
hardships and sufferings he has endured in his apostolic work.

far greater labors: "I have worked a lot harder."

far more imprisonments: "I have been put in prison many more
times."

countless beatings: it is probable, as TEV has it, that the idea
of comparison continues: "I have been beaten (or, whipped) more times
(than they)." See 6.5; those beatings are further described in verses
24-25.

often near death: again it is probable that Paul is still comparing his own experiences with those of the false apostles: "I have been
almost killed more times than they have."

11.24	RSV	TEV
	Five times I have received at the hands of the Jews the forty lashes less one.	Five times I was given the thirty-nine lashes by the Jews;

the forty lashes less one: the most severe bodily punishment
(short of execution) prescribed by the Jewish law was a maximum of
forty lashes (see Deut 25.3). In practice, in order to make sure that
the maximum was not exceeded, the limit was thirty-nine. The condemned
man was stripped to the waist, and then the court officer lashed him
thirteen times on the chest and thirteen times on each shoulder. This
punishment was administered in the synagogue, and passages from Deuteronomy and the Psalms were read while the man was being flogged. Instead
of "by the Jews" (TEV) it would be better to say "by the Jewish authorities."

11.25	RSV	TEV
	Three times I have been beaten with rods; once I was stoned. Three times I have been ship-wrecked; a night and a day I have been adrift at sea;	three times I was whipped by the Romans; and once I was stoned. I have been in three shipwrecks, and once I spent twenty-four hours in the water.

RSV has one long sentence that includes verses 15-17. It is better
to imitate TEV and have a number of shorter sentences.

beaten with rods: this was the Roman legal punishment, and so TEV
has "I was whipped by the Romans"; it would be better to say "by the
Roman authorities" (see Acts 16.22).

once I was stoned: in Lystra (see Acts 14.19-20). It may be necessary to say "one time people tried to kill me by throwing stones at
me."

shipwrecked: "the ship I was on sank," "the ship I was traveling
on went down at sea."

a night and a day: or, as TEV has it, "twenty-four hours." Or "a
full day."

adrift at sea: what is implied is that after the ship sank he hung
on to a piece of the ship's cargo, or wreckage, for twenty-four hours
before being rescued.

11.26 RSV	TEV
on frequent journeys, in danger from rivers, danger from robbers, danger from my own people, danger from Gentiles, danger in the city, danger in the wilderness, danger at sea, danger from false brethren;	In my many travels I have been in danger from floods and from robbers, in danger from fellow Jews and from Gentiles; there have been dangers in the cities, dangers in the wilds, dangers on the high seas, and dangers from false friends.

In this verse Paul lists in a rather disorderly fashion the various sufferings and persecutions he has endured as an apostle. It is well to start a new sentence here, as TEV does.

on frequent journeys: instead of this being taken as a separate item, as RSV does, TEV takes it with what follows: "In my many travels I have been in danger from...."

rivers: that is, rivers in flood, which would be dangerous to cross.

robbers: thieves, highwaymen, pirates; they were all dangers that travelers might confront.

my own people: that is, "fellow Jews."

Gentiles: "non-Jews"; or "pagans."

in the city...in the wilderness...at sea: it is probable that by listing all three Paul includes the whole surface of the earth. It is better to use the plural "in cities" to avoid giving the impression that Paul was talking about a particular city. For wilderness one can say "country," "open country," "places where people do not live."

false brethren: "false Christians," "people who claimed to be Christians but were not." It is possible that the more general sense of "false friends" (TEV) is meant, but this is less likely. Perhaps he was referring specifically to the judaizing Christians, that is, those Christians of Jewish descent who claimed that Gentiles, in order to become Christians, had to submit to Jewish rules and regulations, including circumcision for the males.

11.27 RSV	TEV
in toil and hardship, through many a sleepless night, in hunger and thirst, often without food, in cold and exposure.	There has been work and toil; often I have gone without sleep; I have been hungry and thirsty; I have often been without enough food, shelter, or clothing.

toil and hardship: there is a wordplay in Greek, which may be reproduced by the expression in English "toil and moil." "I have worked (very) hard"; "I have tired myself out from working so hard." Paul is talking about working hard to make a living and to preach the gospel.

many a sleepless night: "many nights I did not sleep," "many times I stayed awake all night."

in hunger and thirst: "without (enough) food or water."

often without food: it is difficult to know the difference between this and the preceding in hunger. Perhaps in hunger indicates lack of food; and without food indicates that because of his heavy work, there were occasions when he had no time to eat. Some take the word here to mean religious fastings, and this is quite possible.

in cold and exposure: this may indicate one condition, "without enough clothes in cold weather." TEV takes cold to signify lack of shelter; exposure translates the Greek word for "nakedness" and means lack of clothing.

11.28 RSV	TEV
And, apart from other things, there is the daily pressure upon me of my anxiety for all the churches.	And not to mention other things, every day I am under the pressure of my concern for all the churches.

other things: that is, other specific hardships or persecutions which he does not mention.

daily pressure: "the burden I carry all the time," "the weight I feel every day." Paul is burdened with his concern, his worry, his anxiety for all the churches. He knows how serious and how dangerous are the problems and difficulties the young, small Christian churches face in a pagan world, and he can never stop worrying about them.

11.29 RSV	TEV
Who is weak, and I am not weak? Who is made to fall, and I am not indignant?	When someone is weak, then I feel weak too; when someone is led into sin, I am filled with distress.

With two rhetorical questions Paul says what he means about being worried, being concerned. It may be better, like TEV, to express the meaning in the form of statements: "When someone is weak, then I feel weak too" (see 1 Cor 9.22). Paul means spiritual weakness, lack of enough spiritual strength to face and overcome temptation. "When some fellow believer is spiritually weak, I also feel weak."

made to fall: this translates a verb meaning "to cause to fall in a trap," "to be trapped," and refers to sinning, to renouncing the Christian faith (see 1 Cor 8.13). Instead of TEV "is led into sin," it might be better to have "falls into sin."

indignant: as translated by RSV, this is indignation against the person or the event which caused the Christian to sin. But the Greek verb, literally "to burn," may mean here to burn with shame, or with distress: so TEV "I am filled with distress."

11.30 RSV	TEV
If I must boast, I will boast of the things that show my weakness.	If I must boast, I will boast about things that show how weak I am.

11.30

If I must boast: although conditional in form, Paul is here speaking of a real necessity: "Since I must boast," "Because I have to boast." Here, of course, he is being sarcastic again.

show my weakness: "show my human weakness." Paul is here being contradictory on purpose. The natural tendency is to boast of strength, of achievements, of victories; he will boast of defeats, of humiliations, of weakness.

So here my weakness must be translated in such a way that the reader does not think that Paul is talking about being physically weak. The incident that he narrates, his flight from Damascus (verses 32-33), could have been interpreted by his opponents as an indication that Paul was a coward. In any case, it was a humiliating experience.

11.31 RSV	TEV
The God and Father of the Lord Jesus, he who is blessed for ever, knows that I do not lie.	The God and Father of the Lord Jesus—blessed be his name forever!—knows that I am not lying.

The God and Father of our Lord Jesus: see 1.3.

he who is blessed for ever: this is a Jewish expression of reverence and adoration. Paul uses this solemn expression in order to emphasize the seriousness of his statement. For blessed see 1.3. Here the translation can be "he who must be praised forever," "he whom all people (or, we) will (or, should) always praise." In some languages it will not be natural to have the statement of adoration or praise in the middle of the sentence, and it will be better to place it at the end.

God...knows that I do not lie: this is similar to 1.23, where Paul calls God as his witness to the fact that he is telling the truth.

11.32 RSV	TEV
At Damascus, the governor under King Aretas guarded the city of Damascus in order to seize me,	When I was in Damascus, the governor under King Aretas placed guards at the city gates to arrest me.

King Aretas: Aretas IV was king of Nabatea, a country southeast of Palestine. It appears that at that time Damascus, in Syria, was under his control. Nothing is known of the king's representative, the governor who ruled the city. He may be described as "the governor (or, ruler) who had been appointed by King Aretas."

guarded the city: that is, "placed guards at the city gates," as TEV has it.

11.33 RSV	TEV
but I was let down in a basket through a window in the wall, and escaped his hands.	But I was let down in a basket through an opening in the wall and escaped from him.

For Paul's escape see Acts 9.23-25.

I was let down: if it is necessary to use an active expression, the translation can be, "my friends (or, fellow Christians) let me down." In Acts 9.25 it is said that Paul's followers (that is, his disciples) were the ones who helped him escape.

a basket: a large basket, made of plaited or woven material. The account in Acts 9.25 uses a different Greek word.

a window in the wall: or "an opening in the wall" that surrounded the city.

escaped his hands: "escaped being imprisoned by him," "escaped from his power."

Chapter 12

Paul's Visions and Revelations: "Paul's Visions and His Weakness."

Paul continues his boasting, and the verb is used in verses 1,5, 6,9. He now boasts about the visions and revelations he has received from the Lord Jesus Christ. But he also speaks of the "thorn in the flesh" (verse 7), which is the Lord's way of keeping Paul from being confident about his own achievements and talents, and of making him rely completely on the Lord's grace.

12.1

RSV	TEV
I must boast; there is nothing to be gained by it, but I will go on to visions and revelations of the Lord.	I have to boast, even though it doesn't do any good. But I will now talk about visions and revelations given me by the Lord.

I must boast: or "I must keep on boasting."
there is nothing to be gained by it: Paul realizes that no real purpose is served by his boasting, but circumstances are such that he must go on with it. It seems clear that Paul really did not like to boast, but the situation in Corinth forced him to do so.
I will go on to: "I will now talk about."
visions and revelations of the Lord: "visions and revelations which the Lord gave me." Here the Lord is probably the Lord Jesus Christ. There is no great difference of meaning between visions and revelations: a vision is the experience of seeing something which is not visible to normal sight; a revelation is God's action of showing a person, or people, something of his own nature or will. In the Bible visions and revelations are God's way of communicating his will. It is to be noticed that in verse 4 Paul speaks of the things that he heard in Paradise, not of the things he saw. Besides Paul's conversion experience (Acts 9.1-19; 22.6-16; 26.12-18), the book of Acts reports several other such experiences: 16.9; 18.9; 22.17-18; 27.23; see also Galations 1.16; 2.2.
The verse may be translated as follows:
It really doesn't do any good, but I will continue boasting. And now I will talk about the visions and revelations which the Lord (Jesus Christ) has given me (or, ...talk about how the Lord Jesus Christ has appeared to me and revealed his will to me).

12.2	RSV	TEV

	RSV	TEV
	I know a man in Christ who fourteen years ago was caught up to the third heaven—whether in the body or out of the body I do not know, God knows.	I know a certain Christian man who fourteen years ago was snatched up to the highest heaven (I do not know whether this actually happened or whether he had a vision—only God knows).

a man in Christ: "a man who believes in (or, follows) Christ," "a Christian." Paul is talking about himself (see verse 7). It is better to imitate Paul's way of referring to himself in the third person; but if the reader will be misled into thinking that Paul is speaking of someone else, something will have to be done. A footnote might do: "A man in Christ: Paul is speaking about himself." But if a footnote is of no help, the text itself must carry the meaning. "I know a (certain) Christian man—I am talking about myself—who...." Or else: "I remember vividly that fourteen years ago I had a vision." And from there on the first person singular form should be used.

was caught up to the third heaven: "the Lord carried him up to the third heaven." Or "suddenly found himself in the third heaven." The phrase the third heaven might reflect the Jewish concept of three levels of heaven, the highest of which was God's dwelling place. So TEV has "the highest heaven." The passive was caught up indicates either God as the actor ("God snatched him up") or an angel ("was taken up by an angel"). The same verb "to take away" is used in Acts 8.39 ("the Lord's Spirit took Philip away"); 1 Thessalonians 4.17; Revelation 12.5.

whether in the body or out of the body: Paul is not positive whether he was physically transported to heaven (in the body) or he was taken there in spirit only (out of the body), that is, a purely ecstatic experience, or else a vision.

The verse may be translated as follows:
A Christian man I know was taken up by God to the highest (or, third) heaven fourteen years ago. I am talking about myself, but I don't know whether this really happened and I actually was in heaven, or whether it was a vision (or, a spiritual experience). Only God knows that.

12.3-4	RSV	TEV

	RSV	TEV
	And I know that this man was caught up into Paradise—whether in the body or out of the body I do not know, God knows—4 and he heard things that cannot be told, which man may not utter.	I repeat, I know that this man was snatched to Paradise (again, I do not know whether this actually happened or whether it was a vision —only God knows), and there he heard things which cannot be put into words, things that human lips may not speak.

In verses 3-4 Paul repeats what he has said in verse 2 and adds, in verse 4, what happened to him in Paradise. TEV has not followed the sentence structure of the Greek text but has rearranged the material; in Greek "he was snatched to Paradise" is in verse 4. RSV does not indicate that it has not observed the division of the material in the Greek.

Here Paul says Paradise as a synonym for the third heaven (verse 2).
It is God's dwelling place. The word means "garden" or "park" and is
used of the Garden of Eden in the Old Testament; in the New Testament
it means heaven and appears also in Luke 23.43.

In verse 4 Paul repeats whether in the body or out of the body I
do not know; God knows (see verse 2). TEV indicates this repetition by
saying "again."

things that cannot be told: this means either "things which no
human words can express" or "things so sacred (or, secret) that they
cannot be told." Together with what follows—which man may not utter,
that is, "which no one is allowed to say"—it seems better to take the
two together in this sense: "heard things which must not, and indeed
cannot, be told," "things which human language cannot express, and
which no one is permitted to talk about."

12.5	RSV	TEV
On behalf of this man I will boast, but on my own behalf I will not boast, except of my weaknesses.		So I will boast about this man— but I will not boast about myself, except the things that show how weak I am.

Paul, carrying on the indirect way of reporting his experience,
speaks of this man, as someone different from himself (on my own behalf). The reader should be able to understand, from the way verses
2-3 are translated, that Paul is really speaking about himself, and so
no elaborate adjustment should be needed here. But if it is necessary,
it is possible to say "I will boast about that wonderful experience of
mine; as for anything else that has happened to me, I will boast only
of those experiences which show that I am weak."

For Paul's boasting about his weaknesses, see 11.30.

12.6	RSV	TEV
Though if I wish to boast, I shall not be a fool, for I shall be speaking the truth. But I refrain from it, so that no one may think more of me than he sees in me or hears from me.		If I wanted to boast, I would not be a fool, because I would be telling the truth. But I will not boast, because I do not want any- one to have a higher opinion of me than he has as a result of what he has seen me do and heard me say.

if I wish to boast: Paul could have continued boasting about
other such marvelous experiences; but they are not proper things to
boast about, so he refrains from boasting.

I shall not be a fool, for I shall be speaking the truth: it is
better to use the form that TEV has used: "But if I wanted to boast,
I would not be a fool, because I would be telling the truth." Or, "I
could boast, if I wanted to. It would not be a foolish thing for me to
do, because I would be telling the truth."

But I refrain from it: "But I will not do so," "I will not boast."

so that no one may think more of me: this is a complex structure
in English and is practically unintelligible. Paul is saying that he

has a right to boast some more about visions he has had, since they are all true; but he will not do so, since that would make his readers think more highly of him on the basis of experiences which he could not prove had really happened. He wants them to form their opinion of him on the basis of what they themselves had seen him do and heard him say. The second half of this verse may be translated as follows: "But I will not boast any more about visions. I do not want people (or, you) to think highly of me because of my visions, but only because of what they (or, you) have seen me do and heard me say."

12.7	RSV	TEV
	And to keep me from being too elated by the abundance of revelations, a thorn was given me in the flesh, a messenger of Satan, to harass me, to keep me from being too elated.	But to keep me from being puffed up with pride because of the many wonderful things I saw, I was given a painful physical ailment, which acts as Satan's messenger to beat me and keep me from being proud.

being too elated: "being too proud," "becoming (too) conceited"; or, in the American idiom, "being too carried away."

the abundance of revelations: it is probable that the Greek word translated abundance means here "extraordinary nature," "unusual quality."

revelations: "things that God showed me," "experiences in which God spoke to me."

was given me: by God himself.

a thorn...in the flesh: "a stake in my body," "a nail was driven into my body." Paul is talking about some painful and humiliating physical infirmity, some bodily disorder, whose precise nature is unknown. Many theories have been advanced, but no one knows for certain what the thorn...in the flesh was. It seems to have been a physical disorder, not a psychological or emotional problem, nor a spiritual difficulty. Some translations simply give the metaphor, as RSV does. Others ·combine the figure with an explanation: "a physical condition that caused me pain like a stake (or, nail) driven into my body." And other translations, like TEV, give only the meaning of the figure: "a painful physical ailment," "a stabbing pain."

a messenger of Satan: "which serves as Satan's messenger," "which acts as the Devil's representative (or agent)."

harass: "beat" (TEV), "batter," "mistreat," "punish."

The verse may be translated as follows:

These extraordinary revelations could have made me very proud. So in order to keep me from becoming proud, God sent a physical disorder that hurts like a nail (stake) sticking in my body. This acts as a servant of Satan to beat me, and keeps me from ever getting too proud.

12.8	RSV	TEV
	Three times I besought the Lord about this, that it should leave me;	Three times I prayed to the Lord about this and asked him to take it away.

12.8

Three times: this precise figure shows that Paul did not repeat his prayer after the third time.

I besought the Lord about this, that it should leave me: "I prayed to the Lord to take this away," "I asked the Lord to take this suffering (or, ailment) away." Here the Lord is the Lord Jesus Christ.

It might be better to put the prayer into direct speech: "Three times I prayed to the Lord, 'Please take this suffering away!'"

12.9 RSV	TEV
but he said to me, "My grace is sufficient for you, for my power is made perfect in weakness." I will all the more gladly boast of my weaknesses, that the power of Christ may rest upon me.	But his answer was: "My grace is all you need, for my power is strongest when you are weak." I am most happy, then, to be proud of my weaknesses, in order to feel the protection of Christ's power over me.

My grace is sufficient for you: "My great love for you is all you need," "My love for you supplies all your needs." Here grace is the power that is present in Christ's love, and which provides the believer with the strength necessary to endure all sufferings and hardships.

my power is made perfect in weakness: this is said in an abstract form but is intensely personal: "my power does its greatest work in people who are weak." Or it may be addressed specifically to Paul: "When you are weak, my power is able to work best," "My power in you becomes more powerful when you yourself are weak."

Once Paul heard the Lord's response to his prayer, he quit asking the Lord to remove his thorn...in the flesh (verse 7). Rather he boasts about his infirmities, so that he may experience the power of Christ resting on him. The verb translated rest means "to come upon," "to cover," "to shelter," or even "to envelop." Or, more picturesquely, "to make its home on."

12.10 RSV	TEV
For the sake of Christ, then, I am content with weaknesses, insults, hardships, persecutions, and calamities; for when I am weak, then I am strong.	I am content with weaknesses, insults, hardships, persecutions, and difficulties for Christ's sake. For when I am weak, then I am strong.

For the sake of Christ...I am content: it is better, with TEV, to take For the sake of Christ with the hardships and persecutions that Paul lists, not with the declaration I am content. This verb means "to take pleasure in," "to delight in," "to enjoy." It would seem that in this context something like "I don't object to" or "I accept" is what Paul means; but the stronger "I take pleasure in" or "I rejoice in" may well be what he means.

weaknesses: "infirmities," "illnesses."

insults: "humiliating experiences," "shameful treatment," "mis-treatments."

hardships: "difficult experiences," "painful experiences."
persecutions: "accusations."
calamities: "difficulties" (TEV).
for when I am weak, then I am strong: this paradox is Paul's way
of saying what the Lord had said to him in verse 9. "I have Christ's
strength with me when I experience my own weakness."
The verse may be translated as follows:
So I am happy to suffer for Christ's sake. I don't mind being
weak (or, sick), or being mistreated, or being in need; I don't
mind persecutions or difficulties. For when I lose all my own
strength, then I have Christ's strength in me.

SECTION HEADING

Paul's Concern for the Corinthians: "Paul is Worried about the
Corinthian Christians."

Paul's concern for his fellow Christians in Corinth is expressed
vigorously. Mixing sarcasm and irony with tenderness and tears, Paul
shows how much he really cares for the Corinthians. He hopes that when
he next visits Corinth he will find the opposition gone and the problems
solved.

12.11	RSV	TEV
	I have been a fool! You forced me to it, for I ought to have been commended by you. For I was not at all inferior to these superlative apostles, even though I am nothing.	I am acting like a fool—but you have made me do it. You are the ones who ought to show your approval of me. For even if I am nothing, I am in no way inferior to those very special "apostles" of yours.

I have been a fool!: Paul is referring to his foolish boasting
(see 11.21). Paul blames the Corinthians for it: I ought to have been
commended by you. The Corinthians themselves should have praised him,
but they didn't, and so he has to praise himself. For commended see
3.1.
It is better, with TEV, to connect "but you have made me do it,"
with what precedes, not with what follows. "I am acting like a fool,
but it's your fault."
these superlative apostles: see 11.5.
even though I am nothing: Paul is being sarcastic. His opponents,
those very special "apostles" in Corinth, said he was nothing. True,
Paul says sarcastically, but I am not inferior to them.

12.12	RSV	TEV
	The signs of a true apostle were performed among you in all patience, with signs and wonders and mighty works.	The many miracles and wonders that prove that I am an apostle were performed among you with much patience.

The signs of a true apostle: these are the following signs and wonders and mighty works which proved that Paul was a true apostle.

were performed: Paul uses the passive voice because the miracles he talks about are God's doing, not his. Paul was only God's instrument in the performance of the miracles.

in all patience: by this phrase Paul refers to the human element, that is, his own persistence as he did his work as an apostle. God rewarded Paul's patient work by enabling him to perform miracles.

The three words translated signs, wonders, and mighty works cover all kinds of miraculous deeds, extraordinary happenings, which no human power can accomplish. In English the word "miracles" is appropriate, and it is not necessary to use three different words. TEV has "The many miracles and wonders"; or else, "miracles, extraordinary happenings, and other demonstrations of God's power."

The verse may be translated as follows:
God performed through me many miracles and other extraordinary deeds among you, as I patiently did my work. Those miracles prove that I am an apostle.

12.13 RSV	TEV
For in what were you less favored than the rest of the churches, except that I myself did not burden you? Forgive me this wrong!	How were you treated any worse than the other churches, except that I did not bother you for financial help? Please forgive me for being so unfair!

in what were you less favored than the rest of the churches...?: again Paul is being sarcastic. Perhaps the Corinthians were saying that he had treated other churches better than he treated them. So he asks "What have I done for other churches that I haven't done for you?" Or, "How have I treated other churches better than I have treated you?"

except that I myself did not burden you: "except that I did not require you to support me financially," "except that I did not charge you for my work." This repeats briefly what he had said at length in 11.7-11.

Forgive me this wrong!: again Paul is being sarcastic. The only difference in Paul's treatment of the Corinthian Christians and the other churches is that he did not depend on the Corinthian church for financial help. He asks them to forgive him for this "mistreatment."

The following may serve as a model for the translation of this verse:
How did I treat you worse than the other churches? By not making you help me financially. Please forgive me for mistreating you like this!

12.14 RSV	TEV
Here for the third time I am ready to come to you. And I will not be a burden, for I seek not what is yours, but you; for	This is now the third time that I am ready to come to visit you—and I will not make any demands on you. It is you I want,

children ought not to lay up for
their parents, but parents for
their children.

not your money. After all, children should not have to provide
for their parents, but parents
should provide for their children.

the third time I am ready to come to you: as translated (see also
TEV) the statement is slightly ambiguous; it may mean that this was
the third time he made preparations to visit Corinth, without saying
whether or not the first two times he had in fact gone there. It is
better to translate "I am now ready to visit you a third time" or
"...to pay a third visit" (see also 13.1). On this third visit Paul
will do what he had done the first two visits: he will not demand financial support.

I seek not what is yours but you: Paul doesn't want their money;
he wants their love and cooperation. "It is you I want, not your money"
(TEV).

children...parents: Paul compares himself to a father and the
Corinthian Christians to his children. Children are not supposed to
take care of their parents, but parents are supposed to take care of
their children; so Paul should provide for the needs of the Corinthian
Christians, and not the other way around. (Of course, Paul is not se-
riously proposing that he should provide all their financial needs; it
is only that he should not have to depend on them to provide his needs.)
RSV lay up means "to save money." The sense is "to provide for" (TEV),
"take care of," "supply the needs of."

12.15 RSV	TEV
I will most gladly spend and be spent for your souls. If I love you the more, am I to be loved the less?	I will be glad to spend all I have, and myself as well, in order to help you. Will you love me less because I love you so much?

spend and be spent: "I will be happy to spend what I have"; the
passive be spent means that Paul will not only be glad to spend what
he has, but also to give of his time and efforts to support himself in
order to help the Corinthian Christians.

for your souls: "for your spiritual good"; "in order to help you"
(TEV).

Paul's question is ironical: "If I love you more, will you love
me less?" The If is not a real condition but a way of asking the question. "Why should you love me less because I love you more?" "You
should not love me less because I love you more!"

12.16 RSV	TEV
But granting that I myself did not burden you, I was crafty, you say, and got the better of you by guile.	You will agree, then, that I was not a burden to you. But some- one will say that I was tricky, and trapped you with lies.

granting that: this is not very clear. Paul is here quoting his opponents in Corinth, and so he forces them to admit that he did not impose a financial burden on the Corinthian church. "We all agree, then, that..." or "You will agree, then, that..." (TEV).

I was crafty, you say: the Greek has no verbal equivalent for you say; it may be better to use the indefinite "someone says" (see TEV), or the plural "some people say," or, with reference to Paul's opponents, "they say."

crafty: "tricky" (TEV), "unscrupulous," "unprincipled."

got the better of you: the verb is used in 11.20, where TEV translates "trap you." It may be that Paul's opponents were saying that the money he was raising for the needy believers in Judea would actually be used for his own needs.

12.17	RSV	TEV
Did I take advantage of you through any of those whom I sent to you?		How? Did I take advantage of you through any of the messengers I sent?

In verses 17-18 Paul asks four questions, which show how flimsy is the accusation against him.

Did I take advantage of you...?: "I didn't take advantage of you!" "I did not exploit you!"

through any of those...: these are Paul's companions (like Titus), and Paul is saying that he did not use any of them for his own personal profit when he sent them to Corinth.

12.18	RSV	TEV
I urged Titus to go, and sent the brother with him. Did Titus take advantage of you? Did we not act in the same spirit? Did we not take the same steps?		I begged Titus to go, and I sent the other Christian brother with him. Would you say that Titus took advantage of you? Do not he and I act from the very same motives and behave in the same way?

Titus...and...the brother with him: this does not seem to be the mission spoken of in 8.16-19, in which Titus and two companions are to go to Corinth to complete raising the relief offering. It seems rather to refer to Titus' first mission to Corinth to get the relief offering started (TEV 8.6 "Titus...began this work"). The brother who went with Titus was well known to the Corinthians, so Paul does not have to give his name.

Did Titus take advantage of you?: "Titus did not take advantage of you!"

Did we not act in the same spirit?: "He and I always act in the same spirit!" By the same spirit Paul means "motives" (TEV), "principles," "purpose."

Did we not take the same steps?: "Don't we act the same way?" "He and I always act in the same way." Titus and Paul act from the same motives and behave in the same way (see TEV). The opponents at Corinth cannot accuse Titus of doing anything wrong. It will be noticed that in the last two sentences of this verse in RSV the verbs are past tense; TEV takes them to refer, not to a specific occasion only, but to Paul's and Titus' customary practice.

12.19 RSV	TEV
Have you been thinking all along that we have been defending ourselves before you? It is in the sight of God that we have been speaking in Christ, and all for your upbuilding, beloved.	Perhaps you think that all along we have been trying to defend ourselves before you. No! We speak as Christ would have us speak in the presence of God, and everything we do, dear friends, is done to help you.

Paul has been defending himself vigorously against the charges made against him. And now he warns the Corinthians how serious the situation is, and what a grave injustice they commit against him by allowing his opponents to make the accusations against him.

Have you been thinking...?: "Perhaps you think..." (TEV). Or the sentence may be punctuated as a statement: "You think that all along we have been defending ourselves before you" or "...that all along it is to you that we have been making our defense." The you is emphatic and should be made more emphatic in translation than either RSV or TEV has done. Paul has been defending himself, but it is not simply to gain the good will of the Corinthians.

in the sight of God...speaking in Christ: the same Greek phrase is used in 2.17.

Here in Christ could be "in union with Christ" or "as Christ's servants." TEV "as Christ would have us speak"; others "as people who belong to Christ" or "as Christians." As elsewhere in these chapters, the plural may be Paul's way of speaking about himself.

your upbuilding: "your (spiritual) good," "your help," "your benefit."

The following may serve as a model for translating this verse:

Don't think that all this time I am (or, we are) just trying to defend myself (or, ourselves) to you. With God as my (or, our) witness, I (or, we) speak the truth as Christ's servant (or, servants). And everything I (or, we) do, dear friends, is done to help you!

12.20 RSV	TEV
For I fear that perhaps I may come and find you not what I wish, and that you may find me not what you wish; that perhaps there may be quarreling, jealousy, anger, selfishness, slander, gossip, conceit, and disorder.	I am afraid that when I get there I will find you different from what I would like you to be and you will find me different from what you would like me to be. I am afraid that I will find quarreling and jealousy, hot tempers and selfishness, insults and gossip, pride and disorder.

I fear: Paul is deeply worried about what will happen in Corinth when he gets there, and so he expresses himself freely.

I may...find you not what I wish...you may find me not what you wish: by translating more or less literally, RSV has produced a sentence in English that is hard to understand. Paul warns them that unless they have changed their attitude, they will find that Paul's attitude is not what they would like it to be. "I will find you to be different from what I would like you to be, and you will find me different from what you would like me to be."

Paul lists the various things he is afraid he will find in Corinth. All of these appear as nouns, and it may be better to use verbal phrases; for example, instead of quarreling, "you will be quarreling"; instead of jealousy, "you will be jealous of one another."

anger: TEV has tried to represent the Greek plural form by "hot tempers"; or, "outbursts of anger."

selfishness: "factions," "intrigues"; "rivalry," "competition."

slander: "insults" (TEV), "slanderous talk."

gossip: "telling malicious lies," "spreading false rumors."

conceit: "arrogance," "arrogant manners."

disorder: "constant disorders."

12.21	RSV	TEV
	I fear that when I come again my God may humble me before you, and I may have to mourn over many of those who sinned before and have not repented of the impurity, immorality, and licentiousness which they have practiced.	I am afraid that the next time I come my God will humiliate me in your presence, and I shall weep over many who sinned in the past and have not repented of the immoral things they have done—their lust and their sexual sins.

my God: "the God I worship (or, serve)." It should not appear that this God belongs exclusively to Paul; so it may be better to say "God" or "our (inclusive) God."

may humble me: in the sense of "will humiliate me" (TEV), "will make me ashamed of you." Paul warns that on his next visit, as before, God will make him sad and discouraged if he finds that the Corinthians have not changed. Their change will be a victory for him; their persistence in sin will be a defeat for him. Yet it is God's doing, for Paul belongs to him and serves him.

It is better to take again with humble, and not (as RSV and TEV have it) with come: "God will humiliate me again," "God will make me feel ashamed of you again."

sinned before: that is, had committed the same sins in the past and had not given them up.

repented: see 7.9.

impurity, immorality, and licentiousness: all of these refer to sexual misconduct. The first one is immoral conduct in the most general sense of the word; the second one is specifically fornication, that is, sexual intercourse by an unmarried couple. The third word means a lack of decency, of a sense of shame, or a lack of restraint.

The verse may be translated as follows:
I am afraid that when I get there, the same thing will happen
that happened before: God will make me feel ashamed of you. I
am afraid that I will weep because of all those people who keep
on committing the same sins they did in the past, who have not
given up their sexual immorality, their fornications, and other
indecent actions.

Chapter 13

Final Warnings and Greetings: "Paul's Final Instructions to the Corinthians."

It might be better to divide the chapter into two sections: 13.1-10 "Final Warnings," and 13.11-13 "Final Greetings."

With the letter coming to a close, Paul gives his last instructions as he prepares to visit Corinth the third time. He warns, he pleads, he exhorts, so that his visit will be constructive, not destructive.

13.1 RSV	TEV
This is the third time I am coming to you. Any charge must be sustained by the evidence of two or three witnesses.	This is now the third time that I am coming to visit you. "Any accusation must be upheld by the evidence of two or more witnesses"—as the scripture says.

the third time: see 12.14.

The second part of the verse is a quotation from Deuteronomy 19.15, which states that no one could be convicted of crime if there were only one witness against him; there had to be two or more witnesses. Two is the minimum number. The translation should not make it appear that only with two...witnesses or with three witnesses, and no more, could a person be found guilty. So TEV has "two or more witnesses." Some translations may prefer to say "at least two or three witnesses." TEV also adds "as the scripture says," to make clear that this is a quotation (see 10.17). "Remember the scripture, 'The testimony of two or more people is needed to settle any case.'" The quotation makes it sound as though Paul is going to take the Corinthians to court. But he is talking about a church matter and is saying that he will abide by the biblical rule in deciding on the punishment of the church members who are found guilty of unchristian conduct.

13.2 RSV	TEV
I warned those who sinned before and all the others, and I warn them now while absent, as I did when present on my second visit, that if I come again I will not spare them—	I want to tell those of you who have sinned in the past, and all the others; I said it before during my second visit to you, but I will say it again now that I am away: the next time I come nobody will escape punishment.

RSV's translation is too closely bound to the form of the Greek text. When Paul was present in Corinth the second time, he warned the people who had fallen into sin before his visit (see the same language in 12.21). Now that he is about to make another visit, he writes the same warning to those people, and to all others who have fallen into sin since his visit. His warning is that when he arrives in Corinth on his third visit, he will deal very severely with them.

I will not spare them: see 1.23. The matter can be stated in a positive fashion: "I will certainly deal harshly with them," "I will punish them severely."

13.3	RSV	TEV
	since you desire proof that Christ is speaking in me. He is not weak in dealing with you, but is power-ful in you.	You will have all the proof you want that Christ speaks through me. When he deals with you, he is not weak; instead, he shows his power among you.

Following the Greek, RSV has the first part of the verse as part of the preceding sentence; here Paul gives the justification for his warning. It is better to end verse 2 with a period and begin verse 3: "I will do this, because you want proof that Christ is speaking through me."

He is not weak...but is powerful: the negative and the positive form of the one statement: Christ is powerful in his dealing with the members of his body. In the context, Christ's power in doing this will be manifested in Paul: he will have Christ's power as he deals with the sins of the Corinthian Christians.

powerful in you: better, "powerful among you."

13.4	RSV	TEV
	For he was crucified in weakness, but lives by the power of God. For we are weak in him, but in dealing with you we shall live with him by the power of God.	For even though it was in weakness that he was put to death on the cross, it is by God's power that he lives. In union with him we also are weak; but in our relations with you we shall share God's power in his life.

Christ's own experience of weakness and power was demonstrated in his death on the cross and his resurrection by God. The apostle repeats in his own work this same pattern of weakness and power.

crucified in weakness: "he was weak when he was crucified," "he was crucified because he was weak." His weakness lay in the fact that he was a mortal human being (see 8.9).

lives by the power of God: "but because of God's power he is now alive."

we are weak in him: here Paul is speaking of himself and his colleagues (exclusive we), or else of himself alone. "We apostles, in union with Christ, are weak" or "We apostles share Christ's weakness."

we shall live with him by the power of God: that is, when Paul
goes to Corinth and deals with the problems of the church he will,
through fellowship with the living Christ, have the power of God. So
Paul will be able to deal severely with the sins of the Corinthian
Christians.

The verse may be translated as follows:

It is true that Christ was weak when he was crucified. But
now through God's power Christ is alive. We, too, in union
with him, are weak. But when we go to Corinth and deal with
you, we will be in fellowship with the living Christ and so
shall have God's power to act.

13.5	RSV	TEV
	Examine yourselves, to see whether you are holding to your faith. Test yourselves. Do you not realize that Jesus Christ is in you?—unless indeed you fail to meet the test!	Put yourselves to the test and judge yourselves, to find out whether you are living in faith. Surely you know that Christ Jesus is in you?—unless you have completely failed.

Examine yourselves...Test yourselves: these two verbs say the same
thing: "Put yourselves completely to the test," "Examine yourselves
thoroughly." It may be necessary to give the meaning of you are hold-
ing to your faith (TEV "you are living in faith") in a different way.
For example, "Test yourselves completely in order to find out if you
are really Christians" or "...if you really believe in Christ."

Do you not realize...?: "Surely you know that Jesus Christ lives
in you!" The question is a way of making a forceful statement: the
Corinthian Christians should know that in fact Jesus Christ is present
in his body, the church.

TEV has "Christ Jesus," which is the text of the first edition of
the UBS Greek New Testament; the third edition has "Jesus Christ."

unless: that is, if they fail to meet the test; in this case Jesus
Christ is not in fact in the church at Corinth.

The following translation may serve as a model for this verse:

Test yourselves completely in order to find out if you
are faithful followers of Jesus Christ. Surely you know that
he lives in you! Of course he does—that is, if you do not
fail your test (or, if you pass your test).

13.6	RSV	TEV
	I hope you will find out that we have not failed.	I trust you will know that we are not failures.

Paul uses the same word of himself and his colleagues: we have not
failed. But there is a difference when the word is applied to him; he
is saying that he hopes that by now the Corinthian Christians realize
that he has met all the tests of a true apostle (see 12.12). "I trust
that you will realize that I (or, we) have been tested, and am (or,
are) in fact a true apostle (or, true apostles)."

13.7   RSV   TEV

RSV	TEV
But we pray God that you may not do wrong—not that we may appear to have met the test, but that you may do what is right, though we may seem to have failed.	We pray to God that you will do no wrong—not in order to show that we are a success, but so that you may do what is right, even though we may seem to be failures.

Paul's prayer is that their innocence will be proven—that they will pass the test and prove to be good Christians. This will mean, of course, that his charges against them will be shown to be false. But he would rather they be proven right and he be proven wrong, than that his charges be proven true and they be shown to have committed all those sins.

The verse may be translated as follows:

I don't care if I appear to be a failure as an apostle; my (fervent) prayer to God is that you will not do any wrong. My only concern is that you do what is right, not that I seem to be a success.

13.8   RSV   TEV

RSV	TEV
For we cannot do anything against the truth, but only for the truth.	For we cannot do a thing against the truth, but only for it.

we cannot do anything against the truth: Paul is here speaking specifically of the truth of the gospel, or the truth that the gospel proclaims, and he is saying that he and his companions (we) are not capable of doing anything that would hinder the progress of the gospel; they can do only what contributes to its progress. Again the plural we is probably Paul's way of speaking about himself.

The verse may be translated as follows: "For I can only do the things that help (the progress of) the gospel; I can do nothing that will hurt the gospel." Or, "For I can only act on behalf of the truth; I am not able to act against it."

13.9   RSV   TEV

RSV	TEV
For we are glad when we are weak and you are strong. What we pray for is your improvement.	We are glad when we are weak but you are strong. And so we also pray that you will become perfect.

Paul is glad to be weak, if only his Corinthian fellow believers are strong (see 1.6; 4.12). That is, he is glad to suffer a defeat if they are victorious; what matters is not his own success as an apostle, but their lives as faithful followers of Jesus Christ.

your improvement: "you continue getting better as Christians," "you will become perfect" (TEV); or "you will be made perfect" (by God, that is). This is spiritual and moral completion, or perfection.

13.10 RSV	TEV
I write this while I am away from you, in order that when I come I may not have to be severe in my use of the authority which the Lord has given me for building up and not for tearing down.	That is why I write this while I am away from you; it is so that when I arrive I will not have to deal harshly with you in using the authority that the Lord has given me—authority to build you up, not to tear you down.

I write this: this refers to the whole letter he has just written.
while I am away: see what he said in 10.11.
be severe: "deal harshly" (TEV). Paul here repeats what he said in 10.2. He has authority, but he does not want to be forced to use it harshly.
authority...for building up, not for tearing down: see the same statement in 10.8.

13.11 RSV	TEV
Finally, brethren, farewell. Mend your ways, heed my appeal, agree with one another, live in peace, and the God of love and peace will be with you.	And now, my brothers, good-bye! Strive for perfection; listen to my appeals; agree with one another; live in peace. And the God of love and peace will be with you.

Finally: "In closing," "As I close this letter."
brethren: "my brothers and sisters," "my fellow believers."
farewell: "goodbye," "God be with you"—or however one says goodbye.
Mend your ways: this translates the verb which is related to the noun used in verse 9, "perfection" (see TEV). So here, "Strive for perfection" (TEV), or "Try to become perfect."
heed my appeal: "follow my instructions," "take my advice."
agree with one another, live in peace: agreement and peace can come only by a determined effort on the part of them all to be faithful followers of Jesus Christ.
the God of love and peace: "the God who loves us and gives us peace," "the God who is the source of love and peace." Or, "God, who ...," in order to avoid giving the impression that there is another God, who is not like this. Here peace is the condition of reconciliation, through Jesus Christ, with God and with one another.

13.12 RSV	TEV
Greet one another with a holy kiss.	Greet one another with a brotherly kiss.

a holy kiss: "a Christian kiss." If a kiss is so much a gesture of sexual love as to be inappropriate as a Christian greeting, something like "a Christian embrace" or "a Christian greeting" may be said.

13.13   RSV
All the saints greet you.

            TEV
     All of God's people send you
their greetings.

     the saints: see 1.1. They are the fellow believers in the place where Paul is writing this letter.

     It is to be noticed that RSV has this as verse 13, so that this last chapter has 14 verses; TEV, following the UBS Greek New Testament, has this as the second part of verse 12, and the concluding doxology as verse 13.

13.14   RSV
     The grace of the Lord Jesus Christ and the love of God and the fellowship of[n] the Holy Spirit be with you all.

            TEV
     13 The grace of the Lord Jesus Christ, the love of God, and the fellowship of the Holy Spirit be with you all.

[n]Or *and participation in*

     grace of the Lord Jesus Christ: see 8.9; 12.9.

     the fellowship of the Holy Spirit: this can be either the Holy Spirit's fellowship with believers, or the fellowship which the Holy Spirit creates and sustains among believers. It may be argued that in all three cases the genitive phrases of the Lord Jesus Christ, of God and of the Holy Spirit express what the three, Christ, God, and the Holy Spirit, supply: "the grace which comes from the Lord Jesus Christ, the love that God has for us (or, that God causes to live in us), and the fellowship (among Christians) that the Holy Spirit creates and sustains." But the translator cannot assume that there is complete consistency, and must allow for variation. The last two genitive phrases could have God and the Holy Spirit as objects: "love for God, and fellowship with the Holy Spirit."

     be with you all: this may be expressed as a wish or a prayer: "I pray that the grace..." or "I hope that the grace...." It is better expressed as a prayer.

Selected Bibliography

Text

The Greek New Testament. Third edition 1975. K. Aland, M. Black, C. M. Martini, B. M. Metzger, and A. Wikgren, editors. Stuttgart: United Bible Societies.

Lexicon

Arndt, William F., and F. Wilbur Gingrich. Second edition 1979. A Greek-English Lexicon of the New Testament and Other Early Christian Literature. Chicago: University of Chicago Press.

Commentaries

Bernard, J. H. n.d. 2 Corinthians (Expositor's Greek Testament). Grand Rapids, Michigan: Eerdmans. Though old, this commentary provides helpful exegesis and exposition of the text. A knowledge of Greek is required.

Filson, Floyd V. 1953. 2 Corinthians (Interpreter's Bible volume X). New York: Abingdon-Cokesbury. Very good exposition, but little detailed exegesis. A knowledge of Greek is not necessary. A valuable introduction.

Plummer, A. 1912. 2 Corinthians (Cambridge Greek Testament). Cambridge: University Press. A helpful study of the book, with adequate exegesis and exposition. Knowledge of Greek is required. Good appendixes, including one on Paul's rhetoric.

Plummer, A. 1915. 2 Corinthians (International Critical Commentary). Edinburgh: T. & T. Clark. The most complete and detailed exegesis and exposition of this book. A knowledge of Greek is necessary. There are helpful indexes.

Glossary

This Glossary contains terms which are technical from an exegetical or a linguistic viewpoint. Other terms not defined here may be referred to in a Bible dictionary.

abstract noun is one which refers to a quality or characteristic, such as "beauty" or "darkness."

active. See voice.

actor is the one who accomplishes the action in a sentence or clause, regardless of whether the grammatical construction is active or passive. In "John struck Bill" (active) and "Bill was struck by John" (passive), the actor in either case is John.

adjective is a word which limits, describes, or qualifies a noun. In English, "red," "tall," "beautiful," and "important" are adjectives.

adverb is a word which limits, describes, or qualifies a verb, an adjective, or another adverb. In English, "quickly," "soon," "primarily," and "very" are adverbs.

ancient versions. See versions.

clause is a grammatical construction, normally consisting of a subject and a predicate. The main clause is that clause in a sentence which could stand alone as a complete sentence, but which has one or more dependent or subordinate clauses related to it. A subordinate clause is dependent on the main clause, but it does not form a complete sentence.

comparative refers to the form of an adjective or adverb that indicates that the object or event described possesses a certain quality to a greater degree than does another object or event. "Richer" and "smaller" are adjectives in the comparative degree, while "sooner" and "more quickly" are adverbs in the comparative degree. See also superlative.

compound refers to forms of words or phrases consisting of two or more parts.

condition is that which shows the circumstance under which something may be true. In English, a conditional phrase or clause is usually introduced by "if."

construction. See structure.

context is that which precedes and/or follows any part of a discourse. For example, the context of a word or phrase in Scripture would be the other words and phrases associated with it in the sentence, paragraph, section, and even the entire book in which it occurs. The context of a term often affects its meaning, so that a word does not mean exactly the same thing in one context that it does in another.

coordinate structure is a phrase or clause joined to another phrase or clause, but not dependent on it. Coordinate structures are joined by such conjunctions as "and" or "but," as in "the man and the boys" or "he walked but she ran"; or they are paratactically related, as in "he walked; she ran" (see paratactic).

copyists were people who made handwritten copies of books, before the invention of printing. See manuscripts.

direct object is the goal of an event or action specified by a verb. In "John hit the ball," the direct object of "hit" is "ball."

double negative is a grammatical construction in which two negative words are used in the same clause. Usually two negatives produce a positive meaning ("He did not say nothing" means "He did say something"). In some languages, however, a double negative is an emphatic negative (as in Greek, where "not no" means "*definitely* not").

emphasis (emphatic) is the special importance given to an element in a discourse, sometimes indicated by the choice of words or by position in the sentence. For example, in "Never will I eat pork again," "Never" is given emphasis by placing it at the beginning of the sentence.

exclusive first person plural excludes the person(s) addressed. That is, a speaker may use "we" to refer to himself and his companions, while specifically excluding the person(s) to whom he is speaking. See inclusive.

explicit refers to information which is expressed in the words of a discourse. This is in contrast to implicit information. See implicit.

figure or figurative expression involves the use of words in other than their literal or ordinary sense, in order to bring out some aspect of meaning by means of comparison or association. For example, "raindrops dancing on the street," or "his speech was like thunder." Metaphors and similes are figures of speech.

finite verb. See infinitive

first person. See person.

formal correspondence or formal equivalence is a type of translation in which the features of form in the source text have been more or less mechanically reproduced in the receptor language.

full stop is a marker indicating the end of a sentence; the marker is usually a period.

future tense. See tense.

genitive case is a grammatical set of forms occurring in many languages, used primarily to indicate that a noun is the modifier of another noun, as in "people of God," "pound of flour," "child's toy," or "Garden of Eden." The genitive often indicates possession, but it may also indicate measure, origin, apposition, characteristic, separation, or source.

idiom (idiomatic) is a combination of terms whose meanings cannot be understood by adding up the meanings of the parts. "To hang one's head," "to have a green thumb," and "behind the eightball" are American English idioms. Idioms almost always lose their meaning or convey a wrong meaning when translated literally from one language to another.

imperative refers to forms of a verb which indicate commands or requests. In "Go and do likewise," the verbs "Go" and "do" are imperatives. In most languages, imperatives are confined to the grammatical second person; but some languages have corresponding forms for the first and third persons. These are usually expressed in English by the use of "may" or "let"; for example, "May we not have to beg!" "Let them work harder!"

implicit (implied) refers to information that is not formally represented in a discourse, since it is assumed that it is already known to the receptor, or evident from the meaning of the words in question. For example, the phrase "the other son" carries with it the implicit information that there is a son in addition to the one mentioned. This is in contrast to explicit information, which is expressly stated in a discourse. See explicit.

inclusive first person plural includes both the speaker and the one(s) to whom that person is speaking. See exclusive.

indicative refers to forms of a verb in which an act or conditon is stated as an actual fact rather than as a potentiality, a hope, or an unrealized condition. The verb "won" in "The king won the battle" is in the indicative form.

infinitive is a verb form which indicates an action or state without specifying such factors as agent or time; for example, "to mark," "to sing," or "to go." It is in contrast to finite verb form, which often distinguishes person, number, tense, mode, or aspect; for example, "marked," "sung," or "will go."

irony (ironic) is a sarcastic or humorous manner of discourse in which what is said is intended to express its opposite; for example, "That was a wise thing to do!" when intended to convey the meaning "That was a stupid thing to do!"

literal means the ordinary or primary meaning of a term or expression, in contrast with a figurative meaning. A literal translation is one which represents the exact words and word order of the source language; such a translation is frequently unnatural or awkward in the receptor language.

manuscripts are books, documents, or letters written by hand. Thousands of manuscript copies of various Old and New Testament books still exist, but none of the original manuscripts. See text.

[153]

manuscript evidence (manuscript support) is also called textual evidence. See text, textual.

metaphor is likening one object, event, or state to another by speaking of it as if it were the other; for example, "flowers dancing in the breeze." Metaphors are the most commonly used figures of speech and are often so subtle that a speaker or writer is not conscious of the fact that he is using figurative language. See simile.

modifier is a grammatical term referring to a word or a phrase which is used to modify or affect the meaning of another part of the sentence, such as an adjective modifying a noun or an adverb modifying a verb.

noun is a word that names a person, place, thing, or idea, and often serves to specify a subject or topic of discourse.

object. See direct object.

parallel, parallelism, generally refers to some similarity in the content and/or form of a construction; for example, "The man was blind, and he could not see." The structures that correspond to each other in the two statements are said to be parallel.

paratactic expression or relationship (parataxis) refers to two or more clauses of equal rank which stand together without being joined by a connective; for example, "I came, I saw, I conquered."

parenthetical statement is a statement that interrupts a discourse by departing from its main theme. It is frequently set off by marks of parenthesis ( ).

participial indicates that the phrase, clause, construction, or other expression described is governed by a participle.

participle is a verbal adjective, that is, a word which retains some of the characteristics of a verb while functioning as an adjective. In "singing children" and "painted house," "singing" and "painted" are participles.

passive. See voice.

past tense. See tense.

person, as a grammatical term, refers to the speaker, the person spoken to, or the person or thing spoken about. First person is the person(s) speaking (such as "I," "me," "my," "mine," "we," "us," "our," or "ours"). Second person is the person(s) or thing(s) spoken to (such as "thou," "thee," "thy," "thine," "ye," "you," "your," or "yours"). Third person is the person(s) or thing(s) spoken about (such as "he," "she," "it," "his," "her," "them," or "their,"). The examples here given are all pronouns, but in many languages the verb forms have affixes which indicate first, second, or third person and also indicate whether they are singular or plural.

phrase is a grammatical construction of two or more words, but less than a complete clause or a sentence. A phrase is usually given a name according to its function in a sentence, such as "noun phrase," "verb phrase," or "prepositional phrase."

play on words. See wordplay.

plural refers to the form of a word which indicates more than one. See singular.

predicate is the part of a clause which contrasts with or supplements the subject. The subject is the topic of the clause, and the predicate is what is said about the subject. For example, in "The small boy ran swiftly," the subject is "The small boy," and the predicate is "ran swiftly." See subject.

preposition is a word (usually a particle) whose function is to indicate the relation of a noun or pronoun to another noun, pronoun, verb, or adjective. Some English prepositions are "for," "from," "in," "to," and "with."

present tense. See tense.

pronouns are words which are used in place of nouns, such as "he," "him," "his," "she," "we," "them," "who," "which," "this," or "these."

restructure. See structure.

rhetorical refers to forms of speech which are employed to highlight or make more attractive some aspect of a discourse. A rhetorical question, for example, is not a request for information but is a way of making an emphatic statement.

sarcasm (sarcastic) is an ironical and frequently contemptuous manner of discourse in which what is said is intended to express its opposite; for example, "What a brilliant idea!" when intended to covey the meaning, "What a ridiculous idea!"

second person. See person.

sentence is a grammatical construction composed of one or more clauses and capable of standing alone.

Septuagint is a translation of the Hebrew Old Testament into Greek, made some two hundred years before Christ. It is often abbreviated as LXX.

simile (pronounced SIM-i-lee) is a figure of speech which describes one event or object by comparing it to another, using "like," "as," or some other word to mark or signal the comparison. For example, "She runs like a deer," "He is as straight as an arrow." Similes are less subtle than metaphors in that metaphors do not mark the comparison with words such as "like" or "as." See metaphor.

singular refers to the form of a word which indicates one thing or person in contrast to plural, which indicates more than one. See plural.

structure is the systematic arrangement of the elements of language, including
the ways in which words combine into phrases, phrases into clauses, and
clauses into sentences. Because this process may be compared to the building of a house or bridge, such words as structure and construction are used in
reference to it. To separate and rearrange the various components of a
sentence or other unit of discourse in the translation process is to restructure it.

subject is one of the major divisions of a clause, the other being the predicate. In
"The small boy walked to school," "The small boy" is the subject. Typically
the subject is a noun phrase. It should not be confused with the semantic
"agent," or actor. See predicate.

subordinate clause. See clause.

superlative refers to the form of an adjective or adverb that indicates that the
object or event described possesses a certain quality to a greater degree
than does any other object or event implicitly or explicitly specified by the
content. "Most happy" and "finest" are adjectives in the superlative degree,
while "least" and "most quickly" are adverbs in the superlative degree. See
also comparative.

synonyms are words which are different in form but similar in meaning, such as
"boy" and "lad." Expressions which have essentially the same meaning are
said to be synonymous. No two words are completely synonymous.

tense is usually a form of a verb which indicates time relative to a discourse or
some event in a discourse. The most common forms of tense are past,
present, and future.

text, textual, refers to the various Greek and Hebrew manuscripts of the Scriptures. Textual evidence is the cumulative evidence for a particular form of
the text. See also manuscripts.

Textus Receptus (Latin for "Received Text") is one of the earliest printed forms
of the text of the Greek New Testament. Based on very late manuscripts, it
contains many changes made by copyists which a modern translation should
not follow.

third person. See person.

translation is the reproduction in a receptor language of the closest natural equivalent of a message in the source language, first, in terms of meaning, and
second, in terms of style.

verbs are a grammatical class of words which express existence, action, or occur-
rence, such as "be," "become," "run," or "think."

verbal has two meanings. (1) It may refer to expressions consisting of words,
sometimes in distinction to forms of communication which do not employ
words ("sign language," for example). (2) It may refer to word forms which
are derived from verbs. For example, "coming" and "engaged" may be called
verbals, and participles are called verbal adjectives.

<u>versions</u> are translations. The ancient, or early, versions are translations of the Bible, or of portions of the Bible, made in early times; for example, the Greek Septuagint, the ancient Syriac, or the Ethiopic versions.

<u>voice</u> in grammar is the relation of the action expressed by a verb to the participants in the action. In English and many other languages, the <u>active voice</u> indicates that the subject performs the action ("John hit the man"), while the <u>passive voice</u> indicates that the subject is being acted upon ("The man was hit").

<u>wordplay</u> (<u>play on words</u>) in a discourse is the use of the similarity in the sounds of two words to produce a special effect.

Index

This index includes concepts, key words, and terms for which the Guide contains a discussion useful for translators.

Index

Printed in the United States of America